MW00979453

CHURCH

AN INSIDER'S LOOK AT HOW WE DO IT

JOHN G. STACKHOUSE, JR.

Baker Books

A Division of Baker Book House Co
Grand Rapids, Michigan 49516

Published by Baker Books
a division of Baker Book House Company
P.O. Box 6287, Grand Rapids, MI 49516-6287

Printed in the United States of America

Library of Congress Cataloging-in-Publication Data

Stackhouse, John Gordon.
    Church : an insider's look at how we do it / John G. Stackhouse, Jr.
      p. cm.
    ISBN 0-8010-6407-4 (pbk.)
    1. Church. I. Title.
BV600.3.S73 2003
262—dc21   2002071208

Some of these essays have appeared, in whole or in part, in the following journals: *Christianity Today, ChristianWeek, Faith Today,* and *The Winnipeg Free Press.* The author retains copyright for each one, and each has been revised for this volume.

For current information about all releases from Baker Book House, visit our web site:
www.bakerbooks.com

To
two Harolds,
Jantz and Myra,
who said,
"Go ahead—*try.*"

Let us hold fast to the confession of our hope without wavering, for he who has promised is faithful. And let us consider how to provoke one another to love and good deeds, not neglecting to meet together, as is the habit of some, but encouraging one another, and all the more as you see the Day approaching.

Hebrews 10:23–25

Contents

CONTENTS

PART 4 FELLOWSHIP

PART 5 CHRISTIAN EDUCATION

PART 6 REVIVAL/RENEWAL

PART 7 DENOMINATIONS

PART 8 MONEY

PART 9 MISSION

V. good vs
discipleship

8

Preface

offer the following reflections to the rest of the church as the commendations and provocations of a loyal church member, not as the flatteries or insults of an outsider. They are offered in love—and exasperation, and longing, and even a bit of pique at times—in the hopes that the church somewhere, somehow, will be the better for them.

Some readers might wonder about my credentials for writing a book on the church. After all, I'm not a pastor, a denominational leader, or a parachurch agency director. Am I not, in fact, an ivory tower academic?

Well, yes, I am. Much of my professional career, however, has been focused on the history and contemporary life of the church in North America. About fifteen years' worth of teaching and research has provided me with scholarly grounds on which to render these observations and conclusions about Canadian and American churches today.

Moreover, I haven't spent all my time in the ivory tower. I've been involved in the church all my life. How involved?

I was raised in the Christian (or Plymouth) Brethren in northern Ontario and attended communion services and Sunday school since infancy. When I was ready, I was asked to accompany the Sunday school as they sang, later "graduating" to playing piano for the entire church on Sunday mornings and evenings. I helped lead the youth group and also the high school version of InterVarsity Christian Fellowship. And I enjoyed attending several Christian summer camps along the way.

After high school graduation, I attended Bible school for a year. There I began preaching, and I have preached in churches from time to time ever since. Most of them haven't been Brethren, however. At last count, I had preached or taught in churches or colleges of the following denominations: Anglican, Baptist, Christian and Missionary Alliance, Lutheran, Mennonite, Nazarene, Pentecostal, Presbyterian, Reformed, and Salvationist, as well as several kinds of independent churches. My wife and I have been members of half a dozen different sorts of churches during our married life.

I have never been a staff musician at a church, but I have continued over the years to assist with music, whether accompanying soloists, choirs, congregations, or folk and rock bands. I have sung in choirs and small ensembles. I wish I could sing solos, but I have been assured that I can't.

I have taught Sunday school at every grade and age level, from tending infants in the nursery to speaking to seniors groups. I have served on the Christian education boards of several churches. My own writings have appeared from time to time in Sunday school curricula for adults.

InterVarsity Christian Fellowship was important to me during my undergraduate years, and later I volunteered on several IVCF staff search committees. I have spoken at staff and student meetings of IVCF and other student organizations across Canada and occasionally in the United States. I have also consulted with other parachurch groups, notably the Evangelical Fellowship of Canada.

I have never pastored a church nor served on a governing board. I have, however, been asked to advise pastors and church boards, and I have taught pastors in training at several seminaries.

While my main calling is to intellectual work, I have engaged in mission in a variety of other ways. I have served food bank recipients in Chicago, evangelized door to door in the teeth of an Edmonton winter, washed dishes in an Ontario conference center, financially supported the work of World Vision, and written letters on behalf of Amnesty International.

I have led small group fellowships for most of the last twenty-five years and trained dozens of such leaders along the way.

I have written for the Canadian and American Christian press, been a guest on dozens of Christian radio and television programs, and occasionally participated in Christian Internet discussion lists.

In sum, there is a lot about the church I don't know. But on the basis of both professional and personal experience, I write out of what I think I do know, and I hope you'll find it helpful to read. I love the church, and I want these essays to be of use to my brothers and sisters in it.

My thanks go to Baker Book House for their interest in this project, and especially editor Robert N. Hosack for his support. Editor Melinda Van Engen has helped me to sound better than I actually do, although I trust the reader will recognize sympathetically that an editor can only do what she can with what she's been given to work with.

My thanks also go to Regent College for granting the research leave during which I composed this book. My family—Kari, Trevor, Joshua, and Devon—have had to endure my complaining about this or that problem in the church and perhaps are aghast that some of those complaints are now preserved here in print. I am very glad they love me anyway.

My special thanks go to editors through the years who have given me the space to try out my concerns and suggestions in their journals. Harold Myra of *Christianity Today* and Harold Jantz of *ChristianWeek* gave me early encouragement and opportunity, and to them—symbolizing all the rest who have been thus generous with me—I gratefully dedicate this book.

PART 1

WORSHIP

1

Music to Worship By

Speaking in tongues. Women preachers. Papal infallibility. Bah! Mere tempests in a teacup compared with the issue that *really* divides Christians. Reginald Bibby, George Barna, the Gallup Organization—the pollsters are all missing the central debate in churches today. It is this: PowerPoint or hymnbook? Scripture song or hymn? Brian Doerksen or Charles Wesley?

First, there is the matter of the actual lyrics and music. And the question here is *not* what proponents of both sides tend to think it is. The PowerPoint/Scripture song folks tend to think that what counts is the mood, the emotion, the deep spiritual feeling that comes from singing a catchy tune and a simple lyric six times in a row with perhaps a modulation up a semitone or two. The hymnbook/hymn folks tend to think that what matters is the substance, the strong beauty of the classic meter and rich prose—even if no one in the church understands what "bring forth the royal diadem" means, let alone speaks in such convoluted syntax as "for me, who him to death pursued." Yeah. Okay.

What matters is this: whether the music brings a particular congregation nearer to God and enables the members to express their praise to God. That is, the main point about worship music is whether it helps a particular group of people *worship*.

Can Christian pop songs express popular Christian sentiments? Of course they can. Can the best ones set the heart free to praise God in the comfort of familiar chord changes and everyday words, with the drive of strong and lively electrical instruments? Surely they can.

But let's admit that there are some real duds out there. Some resemble Rubik's Cubes as they mix and match doxological titles without any logic, anything to make meter and rhyme work out. "Precious Jesus, gracious Father, wonderful I AM / great Messiah, Lord of Glory, worthy is the Lamb." Sound familiar? I just made it up. These lyrics are postmodern pastiche, flashes of this or that scriptural theme that bear no sustained reflection. They're just happy-holy thoughts. We can do better.

And these are the ones in which the meter and the rhyme *do* work out! Some cheat by adding sustained "Oh-h-h-h's" running over several notes, or sticking in "Lord's" and "Father's" every second line or so to supply missing syllables, or mismatching the words and the meter, as in the classic, "Oh-h-h for SINNNN-ers slain."

For their part, the best hymns develop a single theme from line to line and from stanza to stanza, broadening our understanding and offering us new grounds on which to praise God. We may never have thought and praised this way before, but the best hymns introduce us to new and deep channels of praise, and we gladly share their insights.

What we don't need, however, are the superficial hymns of a bygone time, like the 6/8 calliope-tunes-cum-gospel songs that drip with nineteenth-century sentimentality. (You know, the ones that go "BM-chk-chk, BM-chk-chk.") We also don't need hymns with archaic words and unfamiliar music—hymns that befuddle and stupefy a congregation—unless someone introduces them to us with appropriate education. The profound improves us. The merely old-fashioned or the hopelessly unintelligible simply wastes our time.

Now let's move from content to form, and let's reverse the order and talk about hymnbooks first. I like them because they include vocal parts, while overheads and PowerPoint slides never do. I first learned to harmonize by singing from hymnbooks, and I enjoy hearing others around me do so in church. I also like them because they let me muse on the lyrics rather than being distracted by the facial expressions and bodily gyrations of enthusiastic worship leaders. Sometimes there's a lot to be said for keeping your head down in worship.

Overheads and PowerPoint graphics can be helpful too. They do cause us to look at each other a bit and enjoy a sense of corporate worship that way. They're also a lot cheaper to produce (even with, one surely need not say, all copyright provisions being dutifully looked after) than hymnbooks.

But please: Why do so many expensive church auditoriums display these visuals with dim projectors and barely legible slides? Why is there a spelling or punctuation mistake in every song—sometimes every stanza? Why does no one anywhere anymore know the difference between "Oh, God" (an ejaculation and rarely proper for Christians!) and "O God" (the vocative case for addressing someone, as in "O God, our help in ages past")? And why doesn't anyone—in this age of snazzy laser fonts and computer graphics—bother to make the overhead transparencies both clear and *beautiful?* If an entire congregation has to look, Sunday after Sunday, at the same sheet of lyrics, let's have some artists revive the art of illuminating texts and render these slides things of beauty.

We conclude, then, with a false choice and a true one. The "hymns versus songs" choice seems deeply misguided. Don't most of us enjoy both "Amazing Grace" and "Shine, Jesus, Shine"? We do if these are the best of their kind, if they are well rendered by accompanists, if they fit the flow of the service, if they serve well a particular group of worshipers—and if we are not distracted by inferior hymnbooks or graphics! So our choice is to do what we do well enough so that our particular congregation is edified, built up to praise God better.

Let us be glad, therefore, for all the good music we have. "With gratitude in your hearts sing psalms, hymns, and spiritual songs to God" (Col. 3:16).

2

Before You Leap

Most readers of this book do not need to be introduced to Bill Hybels, Robert Schuller, Lyle Schaller, and other well-known leaders in ecclesiastical innovation. Terms such as "seeker-sensitive services" are familiar to many. But when it comes time to consider such new initiatives in one's own church, one can't count on all of the pertinent issues being clear in everyone's mind. It is necessary instead to set out the issues at stake as sharply as possible.

Style and Focus

Consider, then, the two categories of style and focus. Figure 1 shows that these two issues, which can blur together in the minds of many individuals and many congregations, can be simultaneously separate and related.

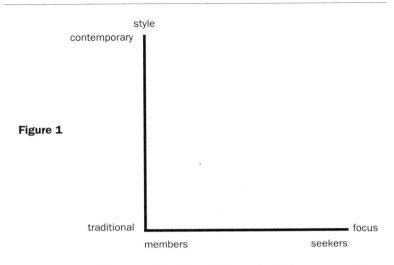

Figure 1

On the vertical axis can be plotted the style of the proposed service. Is it to be traditional, is it to be contemporary, or is it to blend or in some other way mediate between these two extremes? Note that the categories "traditional" and "contemporary" are relative to specific contexts. A traditional Lutheran service, for instance, will differ from a traditional Pentecostal one. Likewise, what Dutch Reformed churchgoers in rural Iowa consider contemporary may well differ from the conception held by Dutch Reformed churchgoers in suburban Southern California.

This question of service style, of course, usually arises in churches as part of a concern for evangelistic outreach. But it might not. The question sometimes can be an in-house matter among Christians who have different preferences. Nor does it necessarily correlate with a supposed generation gap, although many try to present it as "young versus old." Some people in their twenties and thirties might prefer pipe organ, liturgy, and sixteenth- or eighteenth-century hymns, while some people in their fifties and sixties might prefer gospel choruses accompanied by soft-rock instrumentation. Only a careful analysis of the congregation in question will allow one to sort out the crucial question of "who prefers what." Resolving discussions about worship service style, then, depends on who is to be served through it and what end is to be reached by it.

That brings us to the horizontal axis of focus. Here the issue of seeker-sensitive services does come into direct play. At one extreme is the service focused entirely on the encounter of the Christian church with God in worship. At the other end is the service focused entirely on the encounter of seekers with, at least, the Christian community and its testimony of God, if not in fact with direct evangelism and an encounter with God per se. (This is the model associated with Hybels and Schuller, although neither Willow Creek nor the Crystal Cathedral tailor things so radically to seekers; their services are still pretty "churchy.") In between are services that combine these two foci and try to provide worship opportunities for the church while also exercising sensitivity toward those not yet in "the Way."

According to church-growth wisdom, only new or quite young churches ought to consider implementing the seeker-centered extreme. For most established congregations (that is, churches more than ten years old), moving toward the seeker-sensitive end of the spectrum is the most that can and ought to be attempted. Doing more would cause deep disruption in a church.

Thus, we can consider the character of sample services with both style and focus in mind. Service A might be a high-octane, upbeat, charismatic service, full of electrified musical instruments, praise songs, fervent prayers, straight-talking preaching, and so on. It is very much toward the contemporary end of the style line (see fig. 2). But the service is almost completely "churchy" in focus. The language used by the worship leaders is "in-group" lingo; the songs all articulate the affections of a thoroughly committed congregation; and the preacher assumes a high degree of familiarity with the Bible in the audience. Perhaps a welcome to visitors leads off the service or the announcements, but otherwise the entire time is devoted to "family," to God's people meeting with him in worship.

Service B, on the other hand, looks very "churchy" from a style point of view. The three-manual organ, the robed choir, the printed liturgy, the scholarly sermon—it all looks almost stereotypically traditional. And it is consciously so, for this service is aimed almost entirely at seekers—seekers from Roman Catholic, Orthodox, mainline Protestant, and unchurched backgrounds who now are seeking out church. The Christians who host this service do it this way to emphasize an aesthetic, an atmosphere, in which these particular kinds of people can be as open as possible to an encounter with God.

Not all persons of baby boomer age—let alone people in other population groups—fit the broad characterizations of social scientists such as George Barna and James Engel in the United States and Regi-

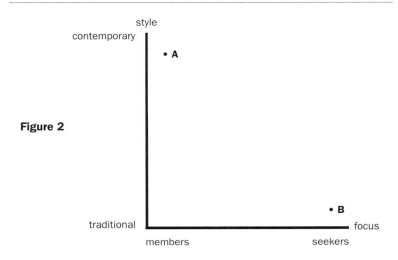

Figure 2

nald Bibby in Canada. Not all churches who wish to hold a seeker-centered service, or even to recast their worship service in a more seeker-sensitive mold, therefore, should immediately opt for synthesizers, PowerPoint projectors, and Plexiglas pulpits. Service B is designed precisely to attract a particular kind of seeker. (I must confess I haven't yet come across any best-selling books testifying to the success of this particular style. But it does work in particular communities. I have seen it in both rural and urban settings, in Canada and the United States.)

Keeping the Balance

Figure 3 is an equilateral triangle that shows the appropriate balance to be struck in the life of every church. The diagram seems to favor worship over the other two components, and different Christians will rearrange things according to their own sense of priorities. But surely no one will dispute the necessity of each of these three qualities in a healthy Christian congregation.

As Hybels, Schuller, and the rest of them recognize, perhaps as well as their critics, dedicating the prime-time Sunday morning service to inquirers means that another meeting time must be arranged for Christian worship. Some churches hold such a service on weeknights,

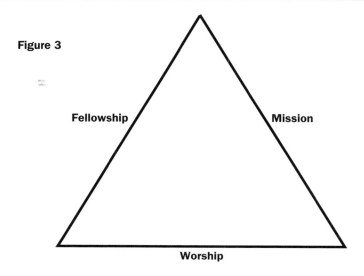

Figure 3

Fellowship

Mission

Worship

but they characteristically run into conflicts with part-time work schedules, family commitments, and other involvements. Sunday morning, after all, is not only the best time for our neighbors to attend church. It is also the best time for most Christians!

Other congregations hold an earlier or later service on Sunday for Christians to worship. But then one wonders about the fellowship dimension. Many successful churches sponsor lively small-group meetings in homes and other places, and this clearly is crucial for larger congregations. But what about adult education, the oft-neglected component of fellowship? Churches that devote their main service on Sunday morning to the middle range of focus (say, worship-centered but seeker-sensitive) can hold a Christian education hour Sunday morning as well. But those who go all the way to devote Sunday mornings to seekers must ensure that all aspects of the church somehow get proper attention.

Some popular writers in our day see things quite differently. They believe that worship is the key not only to healthy spirituality but also to mission. Robert Webber, Eugene Peterson, and Richard Foster, to name some, seem confident that a warm, strong community that is deeply committed to the worship and fellowship segments will naturally attract and enfold those seriously interested in Christ. And in this regard, churches that devote their main Sunday service strictly to worship can, of course, also hold another Christian education hour without trouble that morning.

Others, however, believe that we must be more intentional about mission. They might examine worship-centered communities as various as the Eastern Orthodox and Society of Friends (Quakers) and notice how poor are their evangelistic records. These traditions have much to teach us about deep, rich worship, to be sure, but they seem to have little to teach us about reaching outsiders.

Some may counter by saying that churches don't need to hold public services devoted to this or that concern in order to be active in that area. Indeed, weekly gospel meetings or full-congregation worship services may well be less effective than specific evangelistic ministries or small-group praise meetings. And that's a good point. The concern here is simply that in considering innovations in one important dimension of church life, wise Christians will consider the ramifications for the other dimensions as well.

Considering Calling

A final consideration brings all of the foregoing together. What is the church's calling? Leaders may well have to educate their congregations—and each other!—about basic ecclesiology as a foundation for considering particular innovations here or there.

More specifically, however, we must ask what is the calling of our particular congregation. No individual congregation can deal with every issue, serve on every front of ministry, and be all things to all people. Not only is that obviously impossible, not only is it poor strategizing à la church-growth principles, but it isn't good theology either. Each congregation is a particular community in God's great community. While each church reflects something of the universal concerns of the universal church (namely, worship, fellowship, and mission), it is not a microcosm per se but rather a participant that complements the others involved across the world and through time.

Therefore, we should identify who we are in a particular congregation: What are our gifts, limitations, and opportunities? Such knowledge should lead us to see better where we fit into God's larger plans for the kingdom. Indeed, this sort of humble, diligent, honest, and well-informed analysis is critical precisely in considering the issues discussed above. What style of worship service we should have, for instance, depends on who we are as a congregation: What will enable us to praise God best? Let's not argue in the abstract, as some churches do, about whether musicians ought to be professional or amateur, about whether hymns with rich lyrical content are more or less edifying than simple choruses, about whether composed prayers and sermons are more or less spiritual than extemporaneous ones, and so on. The question is much more concrete. What forms will help us—you and me and the rest of us in this congregation—commune with God in the broadest and deepest worship possible?

What style of mission to choose, for another example, depends on what seekers are in fact likely to come to church on Sunday morning. They, almost certainly, will be friends of ours, not "walk-in traffic." They will be people in the circles of acquaintance of our particular congregation, not "seekers in general." (The next round of social scientific research on seekers, by the way, ought to focus less on society at large, as in "What do secular baby boomers want?" and more on actual seekers per se, as in "What do baby boomers who actually go to church to seek for religion want?")

We evangelicals in particular tend to assume that we already know all we need to know. Or we at least assume that God knows it and that he'll just show us what to do. So our cry is simply, "Let's get busy!" But we often do not think things through very well, and so we rather mindlessly do the same old thing or adopt the hot new thing. Or we spend our time fighting about which way is "better" on the narrow basis of tradition or mere personal preference. Making decisions about worship is almost always difficult; clearly marking out the issues ought to make that process easier, quicker, and more helpful to all.

3

Some Musings
after Sunday Dinner

One is what one eats," proclaimed the nineteenth-century German philosopher Ludwig Feuerbach. We are nothing more than the biological products of what we ingest.

Most people reject Feuerbach's stark reductionism. Still, all around the world, religions are concerned with what people eat. Indeed, most take seriously not only what we eat but when, with whom, how much, and for what purpose.

Jewish kosher laws are perhaps the most widely recognized in North America, but Islamic rules are becoming more familiar to caterers, restaurateurs, grocers, and others who seek business with our expanding population of Muslims.

Other North Americans are vegetarians of various degrees. Some eat no meat or fish, while others ("vegans") consume no animal products at all, such as milk or eggs. Vegetarians might take up this discipline because they believe it will improve their physical health or because of their outrage at what they judge to be appalling farming and slaughtering practices in North America.

Still others, however, practice vegetarianism because they believe it will help them spiritually. In this respect, they reflect especially the emphases of the religions of India. Indian religions typically have strict rules about food because adherents believe that both eating and the objects of eating are bound up with spiritual matters.

Most of us know about Hindu veneration of cattle, for example, which forbids the eating of beef. But another Indian religion has the most radical diet of all. This religion is Jainism. Jainism is a tiny religion: Only a few thousand North Americans practice it, and even in its country of origin it commands the allegiance of about three million fewer than one-half of 1 percent of India's seven hundred million. Jainism, however, has affected both influential Indian individuals (such as Mohandas Gandhi) and other Indian religions, especially through its championing of *ahimsa*, the doctrine of doing no harm.

Jain devotees work to release the spirit from the body through rigorous physical and spiritual disciplines. Their name comes from Mahavira the Victor, or "Jina," who lived about 600 B.C. and whose path they follow. The Jain life is one long struggle against physical comforts and concerns that connect them to and trap them in this world so that they are compelled to return again and again in reincarnation. Devout Jains concentrate on the emancipation of their inner spirit, disengaging themselves from the outer world as much as possible. Thus, they hope to rise higher and higher in enlightenment until they can finally detach themselves entirely from the suffering of material existence and enter nirvana.

In their quest for purity, Jains follow the most basic vow to harm no life. Of course, therefore, they are vegetarians. They also drink only purified water so as not to ingest any insects or other small organisms.

But surely vegetables are also living, one might observe. So it might follow that a Jain should not eat them either. Few North Americans are so ruthlessly logical. Jains, however, are exactly this logical. The most observant among them gradually reduce their diet until they emulate their great Jina in the final act of spiritual victory over the physical. They commit suicide by self-starvation.

How strikingly different this is from the religion professed by most North Americans: Christianity. The New Testament makes plain that the old Israelite dietary laws were set aside by the Christian liberty to eat anything, vegetable or animal. Just as those laws marked out ethnic and religious identity for ancient Israel, so Christian freedom from those laws symbolizes the universal embrace of the Christian religion.

Gluttony and drunkenness, to be sure, are explicitly condemned in the New Testament as self-indulgent and wasteful. Food is a gift from God and must be received and consumed as such. Food is also a powerful symbol of sharing with others, and no Christian is to eat without regard for the poor. Fasting is still encouraged (as it is in most religions) but only as an occasional act of physical self-denial in order to focus on the spiritual dimension of existence. Otherwise, though, Christians have the freedom to eat anything they desire in God's good creation—except, of course, other human beings.

Cannibalism has been recorded in religions of North and South America, Africa, southeast Asia, and islands in Oceania. Normally, it has been performed for ritual purposes, and only priests, royalty, or other elites have actually ingested human flesh. Iroquois warriors, for example, were known to cut out the hearts of brave opponents and eat them in the hope of receiving some of their courage.

If one returns to Jainism, then, one is struck by the opposite doctrine of *ahimsa,* which leads to death by ritual starvation. The Jains conquer not by killing others and ingesting them but by conquering themselves and ingesting nothing. Indeed, they conquer finally the most basic human instinct of all: physical self-preservation.

For all our freedom to eat what we like, we as Christians also have a supreme rite that involves diet. But it is not starvation by doing no harm. It is the opposite: a meal. And it is not just any meal but a feast of human sacrifice.

Each Sunday morning, all over the world, Christians ritually consume the body and blood of our God, Jesus Christ. We do not actually kill and eat human beings, because we know that doing so will do no good. Only the supreme sacrifice of God-made-human will help us, or anyone. So in a manner reminiscent of ritual cannibals all over the world, we eat the body and blood of Jesus in the hope that his life will flow once more into us.

Jains believe they must rely on their own spiritual power to overcome the physical and become entirely spiritual. So they finally eat nothing. Cannibals believe they must seize the power of others to enjoy prosperity in this life and the next. So they eat them.

We as Christians believe we must rely on the spiritual power of our Savior God, revealed in his life, death, and resurrection, to overcome our sin and to be raised from the dead some day. So we take communion.

At least when it comes to these religions, then, the old religion-hater Feuerbach was more right than he knew. We are what we eat.

27

4

Temptation in the Glory

t's no great secret that Bible school students have occasionally sneaked off campus to drink, dance, smoke, or chew—or at least go out with the girls who do. But to sneak off campus to attend Catholic mass?

A friend of mine recently told me that he did so years ago. He liked his Bible college well enough, but he was starving for the high dignity, grand art, and eloquent liturgy that he could enjoy in the best Roman Catholic worship. So off he would go on Saturday or Sunday night, having paid his respects to his evangelical congregation on Sunday morning.

This flight from "low-church" evangelicalism—whether Baptist, Brethren, Mennonite, Pentecostal, Alliance, or Salvationist—to a "high church," especially Anglicanism, is increasingly reported in North America nowadays. In the spirit of full disclosure, let me say that I myself continue to hold a number of views consonant with my Christian Brethren upbringing, but I prefer a good Anglican service to most others I have encountered along the way.

Still, I was given pause by an article authored by a former Lutheran pastor who left the church of her youth and ordination for the Church of Rome. Jennifer Mehl Ferrara, writing in *First Things,* candidly tells of her family's long quest for a Catholic church that, surprisingly, was truly "high" enough. Most of the churches they attended in their first round of searching were too much like the worst of evangelical services: folksy singing without much musical competence, preaching that was underprepared and sloppily delivered, and an overall sense of contemporariness disconnected from the historic tradition of the church.

Finally, however, they found an ethnic Italian parish that satisfied their desire for serious, substantial worship. Reading her account, we might charitably conclude, "To each his own." I confess, however, that I became less charitable as I kept reading. Something bothered me, even as I sympathized with her search for a more formal, traditional service.

Early in the piece, she observes that "Catholics, unlike Lutherans, worship with their coats on, which gives the impression they are making an obligatory pit stop. After Mass, most do not linger to talk but instead race to be the first out of the parking lot." Hmm. And then the nettle: "Obviously, becoming Catholic was going to require a few adjustments, including giving up that Protestant feeling of belonging to a close-knit community."

Well, I thought, that seems rather a lot to give up.

She provoked me further with her conclusion: "I feel I have entered a world with endless layers of meaning with the mystery of Christ in the Eucharist at its center. Here at last the Truth has become manifest. Maybe I am not part of a Protestant-type church family, but I am part of something far bigger and more important—the community that traces its history back to the apostles and their living testimony of the Risen Christ. On Corpus Christi Sunday, I was received into full communion with that cloud of witnesses."

This last paragraph sounded disturbingly like another ancient religion that is attracting attention from many North Americans today. I refer to Gnosticism, the elite cult of mystery, aestheticism, and mysticism that has grown up alongside of, and sometimes subversively within, the Christian church. Gnosticism is all about individual spiritual growth and satisfaction. It is all about contemplation of fine things, sublime concepts, and deep intuitions.

And it has nothing to do with the common man or woman. It separates itself as hermetically as possible from the sort of bickering, posturing, mediocrity, and vulgarity that one finds in—well, in the churches of the New Testament and in every congregation since.

The temptation of Gnosticism is to retreat into a cloud of great saints, to commune with noble and sensitive heroes who have in fact been abstracted and idealized from church history without the irritating and disappointing qualities that actually marked Augustine, and Francis, and Hildegard, and J. S. Bach just the way they mark you and me.

I wrestle with that temptation myself. It would be grand indeed to flee the churches around us for the Ideal Church. But giving up "close-knit community" in such churches is, I'm afraid, to give up the only church we have.

PART 2

PREACHING

5

Are There Any Questions?

've been worshiping with Anglicans of late, and I have found that they have a number of amusing expressions. One of them refers to the common architecture of Anglican churches in which the pulpit is raised considerably higher than the floor of the sanctuary—raised, as they say, "six feet above contradiction."

Whenever this expression is used by a preacher, the congregation chuckles. Everyone knows that the preacher is not, in fact, above contradiction. Anglicans are like every other kind of Christian, it seems: quite willing to contradict the pastor at the door after the service, or perhaps at a church meeting later, or certainly in the privacy of a Sunday lunch at home.

What no one does in the middle of a good, proper Anglican service, however, is stand up and question the preacher right then and there. Indeed, as elaborate and comprehensive as the Anglican liturgy seems to be, it provides no time for questions from the floor.

This is hardly an Anglican peculiarity, of course. Whether a church is pointed toward Canterbury, Geneva, Plymouth, or Willow Creek, it is a rare thing to find time allotted for questions in a Sunday morning service.

For some of us, the very idea of questioning the pastor after the sermon—let alone during the sermon—seems preposterous. For others it would be positively sacrilegious, for the sermon is the Word of God preached, and it is to be received with open, obedient hearts. It is not to be scrutinized in a critical spirit.

Yet questions don't have to be merely nit-picking, fault-finding, or Spirit-resisting. Sometimes members are simply asking for clarification, and no preacher wants his or her words to be misunderstood. Sometimes they are asking for further application, and every preacher wants his or her audience to be eager to practice what has just been preached. Sometimes they are suggesting another way to look at the matter, and no preacher should assume that his or her take on a particular Scripture passage or subject is absolutely true and comprehensive—"above contradiction," so to speak.

Perhaps it is instructive to remember how our Lord himself taught while dwelling among us. Yes, he seems to have engaged in certain flights of uninterrupted rhetoric, whether the Beatitudes, extended parables, or his apocalyptic warnings. But he also frequently took questions from his disciples, from the audience at large, and even from openly hostile antagonists.

Indeed, he used those questions as opportunities to press home his message even further. Far from muddying the waters, the dialogue clarified and strengthened his message. And at no time was his authority as teacher, as the Word of God incarnate, undermined in such give-and-take.

As a professor, I would be a poor teacher if I never paused for questions. When we come to church as disciples, as learners, therefore, shouldn't our teachers there give us similar opportunity?

Listeners might attend more closely to sermons to which they are free to respond. Preachers might deepen their study and curb rhetorical excess when they know that someone in the congregation might ask questions of any point they make. Listeners and preachers alike might have their understanding improved and their commitment strengthened in the mutual edification of the subsequent conversation. And all might recognize that it is the Word, rather than the sermon, that is central to this part of the service.

Such times can also, sadly, give occasion for posturing, provocation, and pedantry. Good teaching about how to engage in such exchanges and sensitive leadership in such exchanges, therefore, will be necessary.

Why else should we resist this possibility? Perhaps preachers are intoxicated with the sound of their own voices reverberating with unique and unchallengeable authority around the sanctuary. Perhaps they are afraid of an embarrassing question, or even a correction, from another Christian. Perhaps all of us, in pulpit and pew, simply fear the uncertainty of an open mike: What *might* somebody *say?*

Yet we cannot afford to perpetuate these two solitudes in our churches: preachers who don't know if their words have connected with and contributed to their audiences, and audiences who aren't sure what the preacher actually meant or whether they agree. Let's construct good, safe, wide bridges instead and look forward to free-flowing, if also responsibly channeled, communication of the Word.

The matter of responsible questioning should not rest entirely on the shoulders of church leaders, however. How well do we parents welcome questions from our children, particularly as adolescence dawns and the questions become more complicated and perhaps more threatening? How do we managers and bosses treat our subordinates in the workplace? Do we make sure they feel free to question and suggest? How open are we to serious questions about important and even delicate matters from our spouses, relatives, and friends?

At a conference I attended on religion and the media, a question came from a Christian believer in the audience. "If we're not happy about how the media treat religion nowadays, how can we encourage some of our own young people to become journalists?"

Now, I realize that the question doubtless strikes some Christians as the moral equivalent of asking, "How can we encourage some of our own young people to become sports agents, lingerie models, or blackjack dealers?"

But the speaker took the question at face value, agreeing that having Christians "salt and light" our culture's journalism is a good thing. So he simply asked back, "What do journalists fundamentally like to do? To ask questions and find out what's really going on. Do our religious communities foster that kind of atmosphere? Does your church encourage people to ask questions?"

6

I Have No Opinion

Ho, ho!" you say. "Stackhouse claims to have no opinion. Doesn't he usually carry around an emergency supply in his hip pocket just in case?"

Never mind. Just listen.

Before I joined the faculty at Regent College, I visited several times as a summer school lecturer. On the first of those occasions, I was invited to give a public lecture and I did. It was a sort of "angry young man" thing, denouncing a list of evils that afflict contemporary evangelicalism. It was fraught with weighty analysis and brightened with delightful wit. (Yes, I am available to do the same for *your* group or party. I do weddings, bar and bat mitzvahs, stags, you name it!) Anyhow, during the question-and-grope-desperately-for-an-answer-without-humiliating-yourself time that followed, a couple of times I actually said, "I don't know. I'm not qualified to have an opinion on that." (It's on tape. You can check it out for yourself.)

It is a good intellectual *and spiritual* discipline for opinion-mongers such as myself to admit limitations and stop talking.

The young C. S. Lewis would grow up to proffer opinions on a wide range of subjects, some of which were beyond even his remarkable expertise (such as marriage while he was still a bachelor). But as a schoolboy he had an encounter that tempered the zeal of even this prolific pundit.

On a country walk with his tutor, Kirkpatrick, Lewis commented on the unexpected "wildness" of the area. "Stop!" shouted his tutor with a suddenness that made Lewis jump. "What do you mean by wildness and what grounds had you for not expecting it?" Minutes later, after several vain attempts to support his small talk with substance, Lewis faced Kirkpatrick's stunning conclusion: "Do you not see, then, that you had no right to have any opinion whatever on the subject?"

The science writer Lewis Thomas makes the same point. "There are some things about which it is not true to say that every man has a right to his own opinion. I do not have the right to an opinion about acausality in the small world [of physics], or about black holes or other universes beyond black holes in the large world, for I cannot do the mathematics."

Most of us will hardly contest the point when made about such esoteric subjects. But when it comes to many other things—no less complex than aesthetics, geography, nuclear physics, or cosmology—we offer opinions by the bushel. And in no arena is this truer than in religion.

I remember watching my doctoral mentor, Dr. Martin Marty, the best-known professor of American religious history of his generation, serve on a national talk-show panel. The audience for such programs apparently just shows up on a given day, not knowing who the guests will be. Had the panel been composed of neurosurgeons, chemical engineers, or poets, I expect the audience would have asked only respectful questions of the experts before them. But I was bemused at how many in this random audience considered themselves to be experts on the Bible, Christianity, church-state relations, American history, and a number of other rather extensive subjects as they belligerently challenged these guests. When it came to religion, their opinions apparently were to be counted as important as anyone's.

What do our church staff meetings sound like? What do our church committees, congregational meetings, missionary fellowships, coffee klatches, Bible studies, small groups, and late-night conversations sound like? Are we to defer mindlessly to authorities? Of course not.

But are we to count everyone's opinion as equally valuable? Also of course not. Some know more than others about some things, and from this truism follow at least two important points.

First, we should seek out and value the opinions of those members of the body who have special gifts to offer us in any particular situation. To do so is a crucial part of enjoying community in a church. Far too many competent people are left silent on the sidelines while the ignorant blithely fulminate uselessly around them.

Second, we should value our own opinions a little less if the subjects before us are in fact beyond our competence. This latter point is especially important for professionals who are paid for their opinions in particular areas. We must restrain ourselves from pronouncing on things in church, on boards, and in other conversation as if we were authorities on everything. And our friends in church can help us by refusing to treat us this way!

In short, some people have nothing to say on a matter, and they should stop saying it at length. At least that's my opinion. (And some would say, a truly expert one.)

7

Tiny Bibles, Tiny Christians

At least twice in his life and at least once while in the White House, American president Thomas Jefferson sat down and cut up his Bible. Using scissors and paste, Jefferson constructed a "reasonable" gospel, a version of the Scriptures that was purged of its unbelievable miracles and preposterous prophecies, leaving only the inspiring teachings of a rational gentleman—indeed, of someone much like Jefferson himself.

In our own day, the notorious Jesus Seminar has produced a similar "version" of the Gospels and has dedicated it to, among others, Thomas Jefferson. In *The Five Gospels: The Search for the Authentic Words of Jesus,* this group of professional New Testament scholars tells us what (little) they think Jesus really said of those things attributed to him by the four canonical Gospels and the so-called Gospel of Thomas. In an ironic symbol that harks back to the red-letter editions of Jesus Seminar leader Robert Funk's own fundamentalist heritage, those sayings that the Jesus Seminar believes are authentic have been printed in red, those that are possibly authentic are in pink, those probably inauthentic are in gray, and the rest is in black. Needless to say, most of this version is black indeed.

It is impossible to gauge how influential the Jesus Seminar is. Certainly many reputable New Testament scholars think it is entirely unrepresentative of current research. So perhaps the Jesus Seminar's much reduced Gospels need not be taken seriously as a threat to the faith.

A greater threat to the faith is posed instead by new kinds of biblical interpretation and theology that cull out of Scripture just those passages, stories, doctrines, and heroes that the reader finds "empowering" or "liberating." Certain kinds of feminist and liberationist theology do this as a matter of course, gathering up what suits their causes and discarding the rest. Orthodox Christians rightly dismiss such ransacking of Scripture according to one's own agenda.

Perhaps the most insidious threat to full-orbed Christianity, however, is the common practice among *evangelicals,* of all people. Yes, a danger looms large among people who like to call themselves "Bible-believing Christians." It appears that we also customarily restrict our preaching, teaching, devotional reading, and memorization to favorite books and themes. Vast reaches of Scripture go unread in our churches year after year. What does Obadiah or Haggai mean to us? What sermons have been preached recently on Ezra, Lamentations, or 2 Thessalonians? Many of us know the stories of Gideon and Samson from Sunday school, but how many church members could offer a responsible opinion on the dominant theme—evident from even a casual reading—of the entire Book of Judges in which those stories appear? Do we all know where to turn in the Bible for Scripture passages relevant to immediate and important issues such as reporting income tax, parenting adolescents, buying a new home, or resolving conflict on the job?

We pick and choose even between verses in the same context. We delight in Jesus' promise in Luke 12:32: "Do not be afraid, little flock, for it is your Father's good pleasure to give you the kingdom." Yet who among us gives equal time to the very next phrase: "Sell your possessions, and give alms" (v. 33)? We like the part in 1 Peter about "Cast all your anxiety on him, because he cares for you" (5:7), but we are less enthusiastic about the verse right before it: "Humble yourselves therefore under the mighty hand of God, so that he may exalt you in due time."

If many parts of the Bible are never preached on or read, never memorized or used, then they effectively disappear. Worse still, even what we think we know of the parts that remain becomes distorted for lack of proper context, lack of resonance and balance with the missing Scriptures.

Thomas Jefferson had a truncated faith and the terrible integrity to edit his Bible to match it. Two centuries later, the Jesus Seminar has also produced a Bible that suits them.

What do our own Bibles—our *actual* Bibles—look like?

8

Less Is More

Preach less often. This has been the frequent recommendation of my Regent College colleague Paul Stevens to professional preachers as he encourages churches to open up their pulpits to gifted lay speakers.

Well, let me add a corollary to that. Preach less.

Evangelical preachers, as well as some from other traditions, preach too long almost every time they preach. I base this sweeping generalization on absolutely no scientifically justified research whatsoever, but I doubt many readers will dispute it! Over and over again I have heard sermons that resemble unpruned trees: luxuriant with ideas in various degrees of ripeness but sprawling all over and containing fruit that is difficult to harvest.

Most preachers are conscientious, I daresay. Most try very hard to prepare good thoughts for their hearers' contemplation on Sunday morning. But most preachers are also pressed for time, and they do not allow sufficiently for the crucial discipline of editing their sermons.

I preach occasionally, so I sympathize. But I write frequently, and I often have editors cut me down to size, as it were, to fit the space they have open on their pages. It doesn't matter if I have another brilliant illustration I want to include. If there isn't space for it, it has to go.

This sort of editorial discipline would help preachers too and would earn them new respect and attention from their listeners. After all, in this age of sound bites, MTV, and fifteen-second commercials, people simply don't have the attention spans they used to have. Preachers must preach to people as they are, not as one might wish them to be. When the cups are full, there is no point to continue pouring, no matter how rich the beverage we think we're offering.

So, as John Stott suggests in his homiletical manual *Between Two Worlds,* sermons ought to be twenty minutes long—or at least they should *seem* that long. And that is *John Stott* saying that, a great preacher not known for either brevity or superficiality.

What if every preacher, no matter how experienced or inexperienced, would undertake the discipline of preaching for just twenty minutes every Sunday for six months in a row? This means each sermon-in-preparation would be timed and ruthlessly pruned back to twenty minutes. I predict that any such preacher would sharpen his or her wits, strengthen his or her powers of concentration, and better engage his or her audience.

I know, I know: "Sermonettes breed Christianettes." I'm not defending those homily makers out there who leave their audiences hungry after eight or ten minutes of thin soup. I'm saying that twenty minutes is enough for most of us to say what we really need to say. We want to render our audiences alert and eager from our pointed preaching, not stupefied and flaccid from our expositional excesses. I myself interrupt my classroom lectures regularly for short breaks, since more than fifteen years of teaching has shown me that even highly motivated students can't keep concentrating on a speaker for much more than twenty minutes at a stretch.

You don't believe me about this twenty-minute rule? You think your congregation would revolt if you cut back from your customary thirty or forty? Ask your congregations, or at least ask your fellow church leaders, if you ought to try it. Or try it a couple of weeks as an experiment. Then write back and tell me I'm wrong. But I rather think you'll be blessing me instead.

Having said all this, I'd now like to address several more things on this subject—ah, forget it. This is enough for now, and you get the point.

Don't you?

9

You Never Know, Do You?

Once upon a time there was a charming little white church. It stood by a minor highway toward the northeast tip of Prince Edward Island, in Canada's Maritime Provinces. One early summer Sunday morning not long ago, the congregation filed in to their usual places, the organist played the prelude, and the pastor gave the number of the opening hymn. The congregation rose and began to sing an old-time gospel song.

In the midst of verse two, the pastor was surprised to see the back door open and four men enter the church. They each looked thirty to forty years old, wore casual clothes, and were complete strangers to everyone in the church. The men took the only pew available—you guessed it, at the front in the center. The church was so small that the four men filled the pew by themselves.

The pastor, the nine-member choir, the organist, and the small congregation all watched the strangers as they reached down and picked up the hymnbooks. A friendly farmer leaned across the aisle to indicate the number, and everyone in the church relaxed as the men all began to sing.

The service proceeded as it always did: more singing interspersed with the customary list of announcements, a song from the choir, and a prayer from the pastor. Then the pastor began to preach, and the four men were pleased to hear a sermon of seriousness and clarity, a sermon that showed diligent preparation and a concern for the particular needs of precisely this group of Christians.

After the final song, everyone got up to leave. The men looked around and found open-faced islanders eager to welcome them. Then the friendly questioning began about where they were from, what brought them here, and so on. The men said simply that they were at a conference in the provincial capital city of Charlottetown, not far away, and were enjoying a day off for sightseeing. They had seen the church at the right time to stop by for the service, and they had enjoyed the service thoroughly.

At the door, though, the pastor probed a little further. "And what do you men do?" he asked.

The four strangers looked sheepishly at each other, and one spoke. "Well, we're all professors of theology, actually. This fellow teaches in Vancouver, this one in Edmonton, this one in Regina, and I teach in Winnipeg." The pastor took a step back. "Well, I'm glad I didn't know that *before* I preached!"

Think of it. You're sitting on the platform, sermon in hand, as the service begins. Then, in the middle of the first hymn, four theology professors file in to the front pew. I'm sure the preacher was glad he hadn't skimped on his sermon preparation that week.

The sage sat back in his chair and folded his wrinkled hands. "Well, what do you think of that, my child?" he asked of his pupil seated across from him in the other chair before the fireplace.

"It's quite an impressive story," the young woman answered, and the old man smiled. "But I do have one question."

"Yes, my dear?"

"Well, didn't Jesus say that he would be present every single time even when only two or three people met together in his name?" The sage looked at her steadily as she continued. "So what's the big deal about whether theologians show up or not?"

The sage-now-become-pupil looked hard at his student-now-become-teacher. Then his eyes softened. He nodded. And in a meek voice he replied, "Yes, my friend. You're right."

PART 3

LEADERSHIP

10

We Don't Care
What You Think

TO: Church Leaders

FROM: Autocracy, Inc. ("The Efficiency People")

RE: Streamlining Decision Making

We are glad that you have consulted us on the matter of decision making in your organizations. We agree that more Christian groups ought to apply hardheaded savvy to their work with ruthless thoroughness.

Because we appreciate your good intentions, we feel compelled to point out at least two important areas in which churches are still not as efficient as they might be. Those areas are (1) deciding on a new pastor and (2) approving a budget.

First, in one recent case of a large church hiring a new senior pastor, the deacons and staff of that church actually scheduled an entire hour for the candidate to meet with the congregation at large during one of his several weekend visits. To be sure, the leaders had the good sense to plan this event in a fellowship hall with refreshments so that no one could sustain any significant line of questioning with the candidate. He could just smile and make small talk as he steered through a stream of people until the hour was up.

Still, however, it worries us that the leaders also scheduled a congregational vote of acclamation. Again, in fairness, we recognize that these leaders did prepare well for this meeting. They trumpeted their absolute confidence in this candidate ahead of time. They also warned darkly that there were no other suitable candidates and that the church would have to wait a long time for the hardworking search committee to secure another worthy candidate—if it ever could. So the matter was completely in hand before the vote. It's just that it wasn't efficient to waste time going through the motions of a congregational survey when the leaders knew that the decision had already been made weeks before.

The same sort of inefficiency applies to budget deliberations. We can understand how church committees might generate an initial budget for the governing board's refinement and approval. What we don't understand is why some boards continue to waste several hours of precious time presenting it to the congregation for approval. We applaud those leaders who run such meetings with an iron hand, permitting only questions of fact and allowing no suggestion of changes, thus pressing upon their congregations only an "up-or-down, all-or-nothing" vote at the end. We also appreciate such chairpersons making frequent references to "how late things are getting" and "how we really would like to get through this" in order to make any individual who suggests an alternative look like an enemy of the congregation rather than a friend trying to make the budget better.

Nonetheless, surely the time could be better spent actually accomplishing something, like raising funds or planning the next project, when anyone can see from the way such meetings are conducted that the congregation is restricted entirely to the role of rubber stamp.

Our recommendations, therefore, are these:

1. Do not hold congregational meetings any longer under the guise of "decision making." Only meetings for informational

purposes should be held, with tight control on comments from the floor so as not to call into question any part of the decision already made by the leaders. We recommend in this regard that the senior pastor or chairperson of the board govern these meetings rather than choosing someone else from the congregation for this role because he or she is not personally invested in the decisions of the leadership and has an ability to encourage honest debate.

2. Do not allow congregations to know what leaders are deciding on until a decision has been made. Failure to maintain scrupulous secrecy will allow others with interest and ideas to interfere with the decision making of the leaders by making pertinent suggestions.

3. When decisions are announced, clearly indicate that the leaders are not inviting disagreement or amendment. We suggest that the following phrase be prominently placed in all such announcements: "We Don't Care What You Think: This Is How It's Going to Be." This saves a great deal of time and trouble as everyone understands clearly the power relationships in the group.

Thank you again for your business. We hope you will also contact us regarding our expertise in dismissing troublesome staff members, squelching new initiatives, and establishing communication grapevines controlled by the proper authorities.

Sincerely,
Rehoboam Caesar
President
Autocracy, Inc.

11

Finding Out
What People Think

The telephone rings, usually during suppertime.

"Um, is this, ah, Mr. J. Stackhouse?"

You know, without hearing another word, that you are being addressed by yet another phone solicitor or survey taker. (How many of your friends or relatives stumble over your name when they call you?)

And it takes much of your considerable Christian goodwill to civilly excuse yourself over the chirping protests of the caller who wants "just a few minutes of your time."

No, you don't have twenty minutes to respond to a "nationwide survey of customer preferences." For that matter, you don't have time to fill out the comment card in the next restaurant you visit, or the evaluation form handed to you by the flight attendant on your next plane trip, or the survey arriving in your mailbox. You're not sure you even want to talk to the census taker (but you have to do that).

At work, people face Total Quality Management and "outcome-based" strategies. University professors have to submit to student evaluations. Even hospitals solicit the opinions of their patients.

Everybody wants to know what we think so they can sell us their products, provide us their services, or get our vote.

Mercifully, however, there is a center of calm in this storm of demands. There is a place where you might never be asked your opinion of anything, where no formal evaluation procedures are in place, where the leaders give no sign of responsiveness to the people they ostensibly serve, and where straightforward critical opinions are in fact actively discouraged.

This shelter from requests for your opinion is—you guessed it—your typical North American church.

This is not true of every church, to be sure. Many churches—funny how they seem to be growing—do solicit input from both members and visitors and then respond to it. But most churches avoid serious, searching evaluation. Budget meetings generally march along with dissent obviously discouraged: "We have a lot of things to get through today, folks, so . . ." A new style of service is introduced, but there is no forum in which to air concerns about it. It's what the leaders have decided to do, and that's that. The music leaders are driving people nuts, and probably out of the church, with their selection of songs. But there is no legitimate avenue in which to criticize their choices and offer improvements.

As a professor, I have the advantage both of reading student comments on my courses each year (even though I wince at times!) and of assigning examinations to find out what my listeners actually think they heard from me. These are rich resources to improve my teaching.

So when you think about the church, ask yourself the following questions: When was the last time you filled out a form to evaluate the preaching in your church or completed a survey to indicate what you had learned in the previous month of sermon listening? When have you *ever* been polled as to your opinion on an important matter in church life?

Most of us do evaluate what goes on in our churches, but when there are no legitimate, positive places in which to offer our opinions, such conversation goes underground, in twos and threes over Sunday lunches, at midweek home Bible studies, or during weekend parties among Christian friends. The energy that could be directed to changing things for the better instead courses through subterranean channels that undermine the church.

Here's my Church Communication Axiom: Communication networks will form in every church, whether leaders promote them or not. The leaders' choice is simply whether those networks connect with church leadership in a constructive way.

Just last week I was asked this question by a pastor: "How can we know whether our people are genuinely encountering God in worship at our services and whether they are sharing life in Christ in a deepening way?"

Being a radical kind of guy, I suggested a radical solution. "Ask them," I said.

Since the mid-1990s, we have heard about the construction of an information superhighway. We can be sure that those people interested in molding public opinion and behavior, such as politicians and advertisers, will be traveling on and improving that highway for their own purposes.

Meanwhile, the local congregation too often resembles an island chain, each island of which has its own inhabitants who talk regularly to each other but have no links with any other island. And on the Big Island sit the chiefs who wish sincerely that they knew what was going on elsewhere, sigh deeply, pray for divine guidance, and then go ahead and plan church life anyway.

Here are a few suggestions to help improve channels of communication in your church, especially between leaders and congregation.

- Have a clearly displayed comment box at the back of the sanctuary in which members are frequently invited from the pulpit to place ideas and concerns. Don't settle for little cards to be placed in the offering plate: They're too small for anything other than quick jottings. (And just why are they often collected *before* the sermon?)

- Give advance notice in the church bulletin or membership mailing of all (nonconfidential) issues to be discussed by the church leaders. Invite opinions and questions *before* decisions are made.

- Hold regular forums, at least once a quarter, in which church leaders respond to questions and comments made by those who care to attend. Public discussion can clear the air of misunderstanding and stimulate further thought among all.

- At meetings in which business is transacted (whether of committees or of the entire congregation), make sure there is plenty of time for legitimate discussion. If you have to adjourn and meet again, do so. Too often participants are pressured by the chair to keep comments to a minimum, thus turning the meeting into nothing more than a rubber stamp.

- Poll your church regularly, both members and casual attenders. Take three or four minutes during a worship service, for instance, for people to fill out a short questionnaire on a particular, focused topic (maybe just four or five questions). Invite further responses through the comment box or in person with church leaders.

- Publish church leaders' names, telephone numbers, and responsibilities so that everyone knows to whom he or she should speak about any issue. This information could be posted on a sign in the church narthex as well as in printed materials.

- Visit or at least telephone everyone in your church in a periodic and programmatic way. And please don't just make them listen politely to your prepared speech about the church. Compose several searching questions that will help you find out what your people are thinking about crucial issues in your church life.

- Finally, invite suggestions from your congregation as to how communication can be improved in your church.

Church leadership is a difficult and crucial job. It is needlessly difficult, though, if communication between pulpit and pew, or between committee room and congregation, is a long-distance call.

Or do our opinions matter only to businesses and politicians?

12

Our Pastoral Brain Drain

anadians often speak ruefully of what we call "the brain drain" from Canada to the United States, as our homegrown talent heads for more lucrative and entrepreneurial positions in America. The same dynamic, of course, afflicts regions within the two countries, whether young people leaving Atlantic Canada for Ontario and Alberta, or midwesterners and Rust Belters heading for the Sun Belt. Yet what about the brain drain from our pulpits?

Consider your church youth group over the last decade or so. Who have been the brightest kids, the ones with the best minds and the warmest hearts for God? Now, how many of them have entered full-time pastoral work?

In too many churches across North America, the highest achievers have chosen careers only in medicine, law, engineering, or business. Many of these people, to be sure, end up serving in churches in lay ministry. But today's awkward question is this: How many pastors are their equals in education, skill, and intelligence?

Intelligence isn't everything in pastoral work, of course. Spiritual and relational qualities come first. But intelligence isn't everything in medicine, law, engineering, or business either, and yet these occupations unapologetically prize intellectual excellence. Does contemporary pastoral work do so?

It used to be that the parson was commonly the most educated person in the village, and his education was assumed to be necessary to his work of explaining the deep things of God. North American evangelicals of almost every stripe for at least a half century now have been requiring more education of their pastors in order for them to properly serve an increasingly well-educated populace.

Several mutually reinforcing trends, however, have made it increasingly unlikely that our pastoral corps will include some of our most intellectually gifted sisters and brothers.

- Pastoral work in a typical church combines an unmanageably huge range of roles: counselor, executive officer, custodian, answering service, personnel officer, social convenor, and—oh yes—theologian and preacher. Few churches provide the necessary time for pastors to read, reflect, and harvest the fruit of serious study.

- Young people see all this and note how mediocre most North American sermons are as they endure them week after week. The youth with superior intellectual gifts come to assume that the really interesting mental work lies in other occupations.

- Young people also observe the low status of the pastor relative to physicians, lawyers, and executives. They note that the chairman of the church board, with perhaps a single university degree in commerce, drives to the board meetings in his Lexus and cheerfully votes once again to pay the middle-aged pastor, with seven years of college and graduate school education and fifteen years of experience, the same salary as someone just starting out at his accounting firm. They note that the pastor is told to do things by the other church leaders as if he is their underling, not their peer.

- Seminaries, desperate for students, keep entrance standards low and let grade inflation mount. Is this too harsh a judgment? Ask yourself: Would an A from a typical North American seminary be worth an A at a school of medicine or law?

Again, superior intelligence is far from being the most important thing in pastoral work. We need godly pastors first, and many churches don't need brainy ones.

But ask yourself honestly: How is the preaching in your church, how is the administration of your church, how is the leading in your church compared to the quality of care you expect from your lawyer, physician, or financial advisor?

I fear that in the worst cases we have the pastoral leaders we deserve, and the good pastors we don't deserve (and there are indeed many of them in North America) too often get crushed by the pincer of too many duties and too little respect.

We might be tempted defensively to blame our brightest young people for avoiding pastoral occupations out of worldly motives. But let's consider a more provocative possibility. Perhaps our prudent God is just not calling our most intelligent young people to pastor us. Perhaps he is using them elsewhere because the typical North American church would simply waste those gifts.

13

Clergy Courage

Not all university or seminary students like their professors. Now, we professors like to be liked as much as anyone, and we are troubled when course evaluations show us that students don't always enjoy either us or our courses. But we remind ourselves, if we are wise, that the point of teaching is not to be liked. It is to educate students: to inform them, to instill academic virtues in them, and to inspire them to fulfill their intellectual potential as thoughtful citizens, family members, friends, and workers.

The great American educator Elton Trueblood once wryly declared about his students at Harvard and Stanford, "The objective is not to keep the little dears happy. It is to teach them."

Two articles in the journal *First Things* once addressed another group of professionals who are troubled about being liked, and they warrant another look.

David Blankenhorn first observed the trend—stretching back at least twenty-five years now—of couples writing their own wedding vows. He noted that many of them drastically lower the traditional standard, offering to each other instead the promise merely to stay together "as long as we both shall love."

Blankenhorn saw such vows as "authorizations for our divorce culture." The marriage partners start marriage as a contract between two people who get married and stay married purely for individual fulfillment. When that fulfillment seems imperiled later on, their very vows entitle them to bail out.

Who is to blame for this lowering of the marriage standard? Perhaps society. Perhaps the couples themselves.

Blankenhorn, however, took aim squarely at the clergy.

Many clergy have, he said, abandoned their traditional position of custodians of the collected wisdom of the churches. They have let each couple start from scratch, reinventing the wedding wheel each time. He asked in consternation, "Why have the teachers agreed to trade places with the students?"

James Neuchterlein, in a companion piece, answered the question. "Many pastors," he wrote, are driven especially by "a poignant, almost desperate desire to be liked. They are eager, above all, to accommodate."

Perhaps their congregations are small and graying, and they hope such kowtowing will bring in younger people. Perhaps they have had unhappy experiences with authoritarian leaders and are determined to be more flexible and inclusive. Or perhaps they are simply "relational" people who hate confrontation, disagreement, or even making a suggestion that might offend someone.

These are lovely traits for certain kinds of jobs and relationships, but they can be destructive for leaders, especially leaders who are supposed to preserve and offer resources out of a sacred tradition.

To defend a long-standing tradition does not, of course, mean that pastors should be deaf to other opinions. Traditions might be venerable, but they are not necessarily infallible. Pastors should learn from the new as well as the old, and not every revision of the traditional vows should be condemned as a capitulation to selfish individualism.

Yet if pastors are unwilling to stand in the mainstream of their tradition to call couples to something higher than themselves, to remind them that marriage isn't just about the bride and groom but about the communities that support them and the God who instituted marriage in the first place, to offer them a vision of marriage that is higher than two individuals getting what they want out of it—then can we be surprised at the rate of divorce?

Barbara Dafoe Whitehead, author of the widely noted book *The Divorce Culture,* is not surprised. When asked in an interview what the Christian church could do to help couples improve their marriages and avoid divorce, her first response was, "This may sound like a small thing, but I am critical of the current fashion of editing marriage vows." There is, she says, a very good reason why the traditional vows read, "For better, for worse; in sickness and in health; till death do us part." Any long-standing marriage will face strain that will test the strongest of hearts and the most passionate of affections. Part of what gets a couple through those shadows is commitment to the marriage as well as to themselves and each other.

High-sounding vows don't guarantee anything, of course. But aiming lower certainly doesn't help, according to these experts. And clergy who cooperate in such diminishment of vows are failing to offer one of the best parts of their tradition: the high call of absolute integrity.

Whether such a call seems "relevant" or "realistic" or "contemporary" or "enlightened" finally isn't the point. We turn to the churches, or to other historic religious traditions, because we want something more than talk-show psychology and soap-opera morality. We want something richer, stronger, and sounder than whatever happens to be current opinion.

Clergy must offer that to us and not shortchange us because they're afraid we'll back away, for, as Neuchterlein concludes, clergy have in the end nothing else distinctively worthwhile to do.

14

Unholy Excuses

once heard a Christian sociologist present some research regarding the Toronto Blessing. Several members of the audience raised questions about the adequacy of her data and the quality of her interpretations. Rather than defending her scholarship, however, she claimed that faults in her work could be traced to the fact that no one would fund her research. Neither Christian nor secular agencies had provided her with the money necessary to conduct a broader, better study. And why? Because her topic was "too hot," she asserted.

Well, maybe—except that evangelicalism in North America has been one of the hottest topics for historical and social scientific research for several decades now, and the Toronto Blessing surely would rank among its most intriguing recent manifestations. I wondered instead, particularly having heard her presentation, whether she didn't get funding for a less exciting reason: She might have presented to those agencies a grant proposal that was just as academically questionable as her presentation to us.

Over a number of years of living among and studying evangelicals in North America, I have seen this syndrome with sickening frequency: My failure or our disappointment is not the result of my inadequacy or our mistakes. It is somebody else's fault, and (customarily among evangelicals) it is somebody else's *spiritual* fault.

Here we have this nice, sincere youth worker, and yet those ungrateful, unspiritual young people won't come to the events he arranges, won't confide in him their innermost struggles, and won't come forward when he invites them to make spiritual commitments. Yet this earnest youth worker appears to have been out of touch with youth culture even when he himself was a youth! One might inquire whether the youth of the church were actively involved in the hiring process that resulted in his employment. Could the fault for this failure lie with the arrogant adults who brought about this mismatch rather than with the kids who have the brains to resist a sincere but incompetent fellow who can't relate to them?

Here we have this nice, sincere campus ministry social evening that we hope dozens of university students will attend. We've rented a gym, put up several (!) handwritten posters with GYM NITE! printed in big Crayola letters, and prayed that the Lord would send them here. Now it's 9:30 P.M., the pizzas are cold, and aside from the handful of regulars who show up for everything, no one came. It must be that terrible secularism on campus! It must be demonic resistance! Or . . . it could be that a clumsily conceived, badly publicized, and lamely executed event received precisely the attention it deserved.

Here we have this nice, sincere Christian school, or this nice, sincere Christian ministry, or this nice, sincere Christian conference, or this nice, sincere Christian fund-raiser, or this nice, sincere Christian congregation—and it's failing. So we look for culprits. Those people over there didn't give money to support it, even though we asked for it. Those people over there didn't volunteer to help, even though we begged for it. Those people over yonder didn't attend, even though we wanted them to. What's the matter with all of them?

Well, maybe some of them got tired of being accused of having a "critical spirit" when they had the gumption in the past to point out mistakes and failures that crippled previous initiatives. Maybe others observed the track record of this group and decided not to send good money/time/prayer after bad. Maybe our nice, sincere Christian project failed because we planned poorly, refused to listen to advice, publicized it narrowly and late, pinched pennies on basics such as a sound system or lighting or a decent venue, and smugly assumed that the Lord would somehow make up the difference.

What we're really asking for, in such cases, is for God to suspend the way the world normally works. That is, we're asking for a literal miracle. And God seems not to be in the habit of performing such miracles—that's why we understand miracles to be, you know, *unusual.*

Most people don't like attending boring functions. Most people don't like supporting inept organizations. Most people don't like paying for third-rate goods and services. Therefore, for us to pray that God will send people to our boring, inept, and third-rate projects is to ask for a miracle. Surprise! He rarely does.

So let's drop the self-serving excuses such as, "Well, we're not going to sell out and become entertaining!" or "I guess there just isn't any interest in the genuine gospel." The opposite of "boring" is not "entertaining"—it's *interesting.* Do we engage people's interests? Do we have their interests at heart? Can we show them how their interests ultimately connect with God's good news?

If we can, people will come. Not all of them will come, of course, but some will. If none of them come, then maybe the fault isn't entirely or even primarily with them. Maybe we're doing poor work.

Or maybe we're in the wrong line of work altogether.

15

Beams First, Motes Later

Homosexual priests are coming to the Christian denominations across North America. Or thus many people hope, as is evident in church votes on both sides of the border in recent decades. Most evangelicals, to be sure, would object strenuously to having as pastor someone who conducted an active sexual relationship with a person of the same sex, just as they would object to any liaison outside a church-blessed marriage. Should such a relationship come to light, most evangelicals would support the removal of such a pastor from office. And most evangelicals would deplore any denomination that might tolerate, much less encourage, such deviant behavior by any Christian and especially among the clergy.

Before we evangelicals rush to condemn our brothers and sisters in certain communions for their unbiblical attitude toward homosexuality, however, we need to consider this little matter of "motes" and "beams." Could it be that right now, in evangelical pulpits across the continent, there are pastors guilty of worse sins than homosexual relations?

How about hubris? Conceit? Arrogance? You know, the deadliest of the seven deadly sins, *pride?*

Item: A pastor of a prominent Canadian congregation recently preached a violent sermon on behalf of his church's staff and deacon board. Over and over, he condemned anyone who would question their decisions, branding such people opponents of God and servants of Satan.

Item: The pastors and governing board of another congregation recently asked for evaluative remarks from the congregation regarding the quality of certain church programs. (Hurrah!) But when one member of the congregation troubled herself to write a long and serious letter of concern, the church leaders responded by asking this woman to *withdraw her letter.* It was, they said, too critical.

Item: The youth pastor of a large church, beloved by the dozens of kids in his program, was taken aside recently by the senior pastor and told to shave off his trendy beard and stop wearing shorts to work. There was now a new staff dress code—in the formulation of which this young pastor had had no part—and he would observe it or be fired.

Item: An internationally recognized evangelical pastor was interviewed in the twilight of his career about his long-time success at a prominent church. One of the secrets he shared was that he sat "on every congregational committee that spends money." Why did he believe he had to do this? "If I'm going to have to raise it, I'm going to make sure how it's spent." (Excuse me, sir: If *who* is going to have to raise it?)

Item: Pastors preach fervently about the worldly conceit of the Pharisees, who reveled in the trappings of authority and power, and then sit down in their special gowns, bearing their special titles, in their special chairs. What's wrong with this picture?

We have put pastors on pedestals, you and I among the laity. Worse, we have put them on thrones. Then, when power corrupts, we acquiesce ("Well, that's what the pastor thinks we should do, although I wonder . . .") or we slip away ("I'm so tired of this guy's arrogance . . ."). And once in a while, we commit *lèse-majesté* and depose him in a bloody coup.

How have we departed so far from the biblical picture of church leadership? How have so many leaders become "like the Gentiles, lording it over" the rest of us so that disagreeing with them is tantamount to defying God? How have we laity shirked our duties so badly that we fail to raise important questions, to expect full accounting from our leaders, and to offer the help our leaders need to make good decisions and see them carried out successfully? How have we bought into this sick, worldly hierarchy rather than a healthy, biblical body?

Respecting and cooperating with gifted, loving leaders is Christian. (And we all know that many pastors are like this and deserve better treatment than they get.) Going along with authoritarian, petty leaders, though, is cultic.

Is it a bad thing to ordain practicing homosexuals to church leadership? Let's instead answer a more immediately relevant question that cuts to the heart of evangelical church after evangelical church across this continent. Is it a bad thing to ordain and maintain a practicing egomaniac?

16

The Actual Pastoral Job Description

WANTED: PASTOR FOR AVERAGE NORTH AMERICAN CHURCH

Average North American congregation (Sunday morning attendance about 200) in average North American town (population 60,000) seeks pastor.

Must be pleasant-looking, although not distractingly beautiful. No obese, skinny, deformed, or otherwise unsightly persons need apply.

Must have a strong personal presence, able to reassure the timid, intimidate the critical, and stroke the powerful. Must not come on too strong, however, so as not to make anyone feel insecure.

Must have solid academic training and must study constantly so as to preach substantial sermons each week, supervise purchases by the church library, and answer any question raised by a senior, university student, professional person, or child. Must not be too "intellectual," though, so as not to speak over the heads of parishioners and annoy those who are defensive about their lack of education.

Must be able to relate to a wide range of people. Must be athletic, able to play basketball, hockey, softball, volleyball, and touch football with the youth. Must be folksy, able to talk cattle/corn/wheat/fruit/vegetables and fondly reminisce about his or her own days in the barns/fields/orchards. Must be sophisticated, able to discuss literature, the arts, and current events and fondly reminisce about his or her own visits to museums, concerts, and galleries. Must be hard-headed about finances, able to talk turkey with accountants, CEOs, and other practical people in the church. Must be terrific with children, able to coo with the babies and debate cloth versus disposable with new parents.

Must be psychologically adept to handle anyone who desires counseling, from young couples considering marriage to older couples considering divorce, from adolescents coping with sexual temptation to adults coping with sexual abuse, and from parents concerned about their growing children to children concerned about their aging parents.

Must be well versed in music (both classical and contemporary), poetry, drama, and liturgy so as to direct all worship services. Must be able to select three or four songs each week for congregational singing that perfectly match the day's readings and sermon subject. Must be able to sort out conflicts gracefully among the organist, worship leader, choir director, and youth band.

Must be a brilliant teacher: witty yet reverent, profound yet simple, and erudite yet humble—whether teaching kindergartners in Vacation Bible School, young people at camp, or seniors in Sunday school. Must always be ready to step in when, on Saturday night or Sunday morning, a teacher phones to say he or she can't show up for class.

Must have an infinitely flexible schedule to allow for interruptions by phone or visit, at work or home, day or night; to see parishioners at their request but also at their convenience; and to attend every function of the church so that no one feels the event is unimportant to the pastor.

Must be politically astute so as to cope with constant criticism and to fend off periodic attempts at ouster or wage reduction. Must know how to prepare to jump ship to another church just before being cast adrift with two weeks' notice in the middle of the winter.

Must work for a living wage with a few other benefits: nothing fancy, of course, since pastors, after all, are spiritual people—and, let's face it, what do they do all day anyhow?

This is the "Renaissance Man or Woman" model of church leadership. It is rarely admitted to but widely applied all over North America, and it is simply impossible to sustain without terrible cost to pastors, their families, and their churches.

Worse still, it is unbiblical. It contradicts the image of the body of Christ, the doctrine of the priesthood of all believers, the dignity of the pastoral office, and the call of every person—not just a hired hand or two—to ministry. What *we* want in a pastor is not important. What *God* wants in a *church* is all-important.

17

Creativity and Pastoral Leadership

Every perfect gift is from above, coming down from the Father of lights.

James 1:17

"The really important thing, and the really tough thing, is asking a good question." That sentence is one of the sagest bits of academic advice I have ever received. The gist of it came from Mark Noll, who taught me at the Wheaton College Graduate School twenty years ago.

Coming up with an unusual, interesting, and important question that can provoke and guide one's research is the crucial challenge in scholarship and in many of life's pursuits. "The rest," Professor Noll has reminded me with a small smile, "is just work."

Creativity largely consists of asking good questions and then sorting out the best answer from the many possible solutions to the problem. But how does one go about formulating a good question and recognizing a good answer?

About ten years ago, University of Chicago psychologist Mihaly Csikszentmihalyi directed his team of researchers to interview more than ninety people who were nearing the end of outstandingly creative careers: Nobel Prize winners, Pulitzer Prize winners, poets laureate, executives of major corporations and charities, and the like.

As he and his team probed the testimonies of these unusually influential people, they found that no one could be "creative" on demand. All of the good ideas these people had offered to the world, they said, had simply come to them, often in decidedly "nonintellectual" places and times.

Many of them got their best ideas while walking their dogs, gardening, washing dishes, or (especially) while slowly waking up in the morning. More than a few reported solving difficult challenges in their dreams.

Perhaps the best story of all comes from Alan Kay, whose inventions revolutionized personal computers. He claimed that the company he worked for lost tens of millions of dollars by refusing to install a fourteen-thousand-dollar shower stall in a corner of his office—because most of his new ideas came while he showered.

All one can do, these outstandingly creative people agreed, is arrange one's life as best as one can so one can be most receptive to new ideas. One must cultivate one's intellectual soil and then simply hope that fruitful ideas arise. There seems to be no technique that will automatically generate new, good ideas.

The apostle Paul understood this principle when it came to spiritual creativity as well. As he berated the Corinthians for crediting their favorite pastors with this or that ecclesiastical success, Paul set things straight: "I planted, Apollos watered, but God gave the growth. So neither the one who plants nor the one who waters is anything, but only God who gives the growth" (1 Cor. 3:6–7).

C. S. Lewis was arguably one of the most creative writers of the twentieth century. Among his several remarkable gifts was his talent for images, for illustrations that made profound things clear and convincing. Most of us recall Venusian landscapes and Martian species from his space trilogy, or homey instances of everyday temptation from *The Screwtape Letters,* or the almost unbearably brilliant heaven in *The Great Divorce,* or even brief word pictures from *Mere Christianity,* such as the Author sitting "outside" the time line of his novel while putting himself as a character within it—Lewis's metaphor of the incarnation. Almost all of us, of course, have met the great Aslan, never to forget him.

Lewis testified that he just saw such things in his head and then wrote them down. In his last year or so of life, however, as he suffered from several debilities, he quietly announced to a friend that he did not expect to write anything new. The pictures, he said, had stopped.

After fifteen years of teaching, I have concluded that I have no idea how to teach students how to ask really good questions because I don't know how to produce them myself. I can show them how to weed out bad questions, how to refine the questions they have, and how to go about answering their questions. But I cannot show them how to think creatively.

All we can do is do what we can. We can arrange our lives, our work spaces, our schedules, our intellectual and spiritual diets, and our company to stimulate freshness, to encourage innovation, and to welcome the unusual. We can seek out new experiences, listen to unusual opinions, and read magazines, books, and web sites that we normally wouldn't give more than a glance.

We also can develop the critical tools necessary to separate the precious wheat from the copious chaff that all creative people develop along the way to a really good idea. We can enlist friends to help us in this work, especially as they are not as attached to our ideas as we are and can more ruthlessly set the inferior ones aside. Like a faithful farmer who doesn't just idly wait for God to rain down a harvest or make manna appear in the morning, we can diligently do our job and trust God to do his.

But the pictures either appear or they don't. The insights flash across our minds like God's own lightning or they don't. The green shoots emerge or they don't.

Johann Sebastian Bach recognized this truth and often wrote "J.J." at the top of a new sheet of staff paper as he began a composition. In German, it meant, "Jesus help me." If Bach himself needed divine assistance, how much more do we!

Jesus' brother James reminds us: "If any of you is lacking wisdom, ask God, who gives to all generously and ungrudgingly, and it will be given you" (James 1:5).

There is no guaranteed way to be creative—in business, in parenting, in pastoral work, in anything. Creative questions and fruitful answers, then, will most likely arise when we start with the best question of all: "Lord, will you please help?"

PART 4

FELLOWSHIP

18

Are You a Member?

As it is, there are many members, yet one body. The eye cannot say to the hand, "I have no need of you," nor again the head to the feet, "I have no need of you." On the contrary, the members of the body that seem to be weaker are indispensable, and those members of the body that we think less honorable we clothe with greater honor, and our less respectable members are treated with greater respect; whereas our more respectable members do not need this. But God has so arranged the body, giving the greater honor to the inferior member, that there may be no dissension within the body, but the members may have the same care for one another. If one member suffers, all suffer together with it; if one member is honored, all rejoice together with it. Now you are the body of Christ and individually members of it.

1 Corinthians 12:20–27

Some of us in church on a given Sunday morning are visitors. Some of us are members—but we're not really members. Others of us are not members—but in some ways we *are* members.

To say it somewhat differently: Some of us are members—but we're really not members, and we should decide either to be members or not to be members. Others of us are not members, but we are members, so we really ought to become members.

Got that?

The New Testament presents to us groups of Christians in various locales, groups that were called "churches": "gatherings" or "assemblies" of Christians. The New Testament assumes that Christians belonged to such gatherings: If one was a Christian, one was part of the church, and that normally meant that one was then a member of a particular local assembly of fellow Christians. This understanding of membership had nothing to do with formal status, nothing to do with certificates printed on good stock or names on church rolls, nothing "official." Members were members as a matter of identity with and participation in the group of Christians that was the local manifestation of the body of Christ.

This concept of membership is quite rich. A Christian is a participant, an instrument, a person to be cared for by the others, and a person to care for the others as he or she is gifted and called by God to do so. A Christian is fully involved in the church's activities of worship (concentrating on God), fellowship (concentrating on one another), and mission (concentrating on the needy world).

Paul's favorite image of the church is the human body. He points to its diversity and its unity; each member is both necessary and different from the others. Each member is an individual, but each also finds his or her true identity and fulfillment in the functioning of the whole body.

There simply is no such thing in the Bible as an "independent," Lone Ranger Christian who has no allegiance to a particular church. There also is no such thing as a merely formal, official church member who in fact contributes little or nothing to the common enterprise of the congregation.

In most churches, we see three categories of church attenders:

- *Visitors,* from whom nothing is expected except common courtesy as they attend our meetings and to whom little is given except whatever benefit those meetings give them—plus the occasional emergency aid to those in need.

- *Members,* from whom we expect consistent and vigorous involvement—from prayer for the church, to work in the church, to giving money to the church, to enjoyment of the church— and to whom all the resources of the church are open: for friendship, casual socializing, rewarding labor, artistic projects, emergency financial aid and advice, counseling, worship, and so on.
- *Adherents,* those among us who are consistently involved in the church, who identify themselves with us by their attendance and other activity, but who have not entered into the commitment of membership.

I must confess that I find the category of "adherents" to be an odd category indeed. Certainly there is no direct parallel for it in the New Testament. (It reminds me a little of the Gentile "God fearers" on the periphery of the Jewish synagogue. But clearly they are not a parallel for the church, since adherents are indeed fully Christian believers, not second-class believers of some sort.)

I suppose one could see this status as a transitional phase, as one moves from "visitor" to "member," becoming increasingly familiar with the church and its Lord and taking more and more on board until one is ready to join the company of believers. But I cannot find a New Testament pattern for "adherence" that corresponds with what it is for many North Americans: a more-or-less permanent wait-and-see, second-class *commitment* to the church.

Now, some adherents are members in everything but name. They work, pray, give, and enjoy the church to the full. But their formal membership is "back home," perhaps, in the church of their youth. Or they don't see any reason to bother with formal membership per se.

In regard to the former case, let's observe that sentimental church membership is not a biblical idea. You *are* a member where you are *in fact* a member, and formal membership therefore should simply be a declaration of lived reality.

In the latter, if formal membership doesn't seem worth bothering about, why don't you just go ahead and join? Why not declare the reality of your commitment? If you do, the church can formally keep track of you for pastoral care; the church doesn't have to be embarrassed about asking you for help with church projects; and the church will recognize its full commitment to you in times of trouble. It simply makes a helpful difference if you declare your commitment clearly.

For some of us, perhaps, taking such a step is like moving from living together in common-law marriage to the legal declaration of marriage. In both sides of the analogy, people recognize at some level, although perhaps unconsciously, that there is in fact an important difference between the one form of shared life and the other. Such adherents tend to take commitment seriously, so seriously that they don't want to commit to a particular congregation, to identify themselves with this group of troubled, confused, irritating, stumbling Christians. They recognize that every church, and this church in particular, has serious problems, and they want to make sure they really want to belong and take the rest of us fully on board before they finally commit themselves in membership.

In a culture that prizes individual autonomy and freedom and that deprecates corporate commitments, this makes a lot of sense. But it is not a biblical idea.

We are stuck with the church. The old saying "You can choose your friends, but you can't choose your family" applies also to the family of God. In cities in which there are dozens of Christian churches, people believe they really can choose their church. But the family of God is always and everywhere made up of fallible, shortsighted, struggling human beings bound together ultimately only by their common allegiance to Jesus and their commitment to each other in service to him. There is no other kind of church to choose.

Eugene Peterson writes:

Churches are not Victorian parlors where everything is always picked up and ready for guests. They are messy family rooms. . . . Things are out of order, to be sure, but that is what happens to churches that are lived in. They are not show rooms. They are living rooms, and if the persons living in them are sinners, there are going to be clothes scattered about, handprints on the woodwork, and mud on the carpet. For as long as Jesus insists on calling sinners and not the righteous to repentance—and there is no indication as yet that he has changed his policy in that regard—churches are going to be an embarrassment to the fastidious and an affront to the upright. [Churches are] *lampstands:* they are places, locations, where the light of Christ is shown. They are not themselves the light. There is nothing particularly

glamorous about churches, nor, on the other hand, is there anything particularly shameful about them. They simply are.

Some churches are healthier than others. Some offer us better
opportunities for worship, fellowship, and mission than others. And
each is just different from the others, with some simply appealing to
us more and others less. So there is nothing obviously wrong about
visiting different churches to see where God would place us. Rather
than engaging in "church shopping," that is, we engage in a "church
search."

Once we have found a congenial church, a church we can respect
and that welcomes us, however, how long can we justify staying in
the limbo of "adherent" status? What reasons can we give to justify
committing ourselves a little, or a lot, but not entirely?

We are, like it or not, members of the body of Christ. Furthermore,
the assumption as well as the clear teaching of the New Testament is
that we are not members simply of the universal body of Christ. Our
membership in the body of Christ is always expressed in the concrete,
particular instance of membership in a particular congregation. There
are no free-floating members, committed only to a vague, ideal, universal church.

English archbishop William Temple once put this sarcastically: "I
believe in one holy, infallible church of which, I regret to say, at the
present time I am the only member." There are just real members
committed to real churches, and then there is everybody else not so
committed.

So here is the exhortation to adherents: If the church you currently
attend offends you or otherwise seems deeply wrong for you, then
you are right to consider whether God wants you to move on. But as
long as it is a truly Christian church, as long as it is a congregation that
loves you and wants to enlist you in full-time commitment to Christ,
as long as it is on the right way toward maturity—whatever its faults
at present—then why hold back?

Some of us aren't members but are involved in the church body
and soul. The Bible makes no distinction between official membership and practical membership, but we North Americans tend to do
so! If you aren't a member (officially), but you really are a member
(practically), it is time to consider seriously whether you ought to take
the steps necessary in your particular congregation to join up fully—
to the encouragement of all.

As for members, prepare now to be made uncomfortable as well! It is a sinful irony that some of us members don't take membership as seriously as do the adherents who hesitate over it. We're content with formal membership—just don't ask us to *act* like members. Don't ask us to give much time to the church; don't ask us to give much money; don't ask us to give much attention to the church's needs and successes.

Don't expect us to pray regularly for the leaders of the church. Don't expect us to attend anything that isn't convenient to our schedules. Don't expect us to stay informed about church life in order to vote intelligently at church meetings. Don't expect us to curb our critical tongues out of loyalty to the church. Don't expect us to work hard for peace among members. Don't expect us to do anything we don't feel like doing. Don't expect us really to act like members. You've got our names on the roll, our bodies in the pews, our tithes from time to time—what more do you want?

The Bible knows nothing of mere formal membership—whether in the kingdom of God or in a local church. Membership is as membership does. Some of us are members, but we're not really members, and we had better decide whether we are going to act like members or face reality and give up the pretense.

Let's have no more division between profession and action, between halfway and all-the-way commitments. Members, Jesus commands us to act like members! Adherents, listen to hear whether God calls you now to adhere more closely in the covenant of formal, committed congregational membership.

No church can properly say to you, "We don't really need you. Join if you like. Participate if you want to. But we're just fine either way." We are *not* fine without you. Exciting and important opportunities are before each congregation, and some of them cannot be grasped because we don't have enough true members to exploit them. Most churches currently suffer already in this area or that because they lack enough committed, authentic members.

Is it time to put the book down and call the church office?

19

We Need More Arguments

In one of Monty Python's classic sketches, comedians Michael Palin and John Cleese confront each other across a desk in a nondescript office. Palin is the ordinary bloke, while Cleese is the irritating Oxbridgean with the impossibly posh accent and infuriatingly frozen visage. Palin has begun by popping his head in the door and cheerily asking, "Is this the room for an argument?"

Cleese replies superciliously, "I told you once."

The surprised Palin responds, "No, you didn't!"

"I most certainly did," Cleese maintains.

Palin enters the room, now thoroughly embroiled in the exchange, and the two men continue in this vein, to Palin's mounting frustration. Cleese simply contradicts everything Palin says.

Back and forth the nonsense goes until finally Palin shouts, "This isn't an argument! An argument is a series of propositions laid out in order to establish a central point. It's *not* the mere gainsaying of whatever the other person says!"

To this, after a precise comedic pause, Cleese loftily replies, "*Can* be."

With this classic text resonating in our minds, then, I offer the following declaration: We need more arguments in our churches, in our families, in our marriages, in our schools, in our country, in our lives.

Let me rush to say that we don't need more bickering. We all have plenty of that already. We certainly don't need more contention, more backbiting, more disrespect, and more denunciations.

What we do need instead is more proper argument. Proper argument sets out as clearly as possible just why someone has come to a particular conclusion. It exposes the evidence for this conclusion and shows all the steps by which the person arrived at this opinion.

Proper argument, then, invites the listener or reader to scrutinize both the warrants and the logic of the argument. Perhaps the warrants are weak at step B: "The Bible tells the truth (step A); the Bible says that God helps those who help themselves (step B—a highly questionable claim about the Bible's teaching!); therefore, we should do what we can to help ourselves (step C)."

Perhaps the argument leaps from step D to step F with no intermediate step E: "Since God commanded Adam and Eve to eat only green plants (step D), we should be vegetarians (step F)." This argument leaves out step E, which would have to demonstrate that what God commanded regarding diet in the Garden of Eden is entirely applicable to Christians today.

The listener or reader follows the argument and then offers whatever he or she can to complement, correct, or replace the argument. From there, the process circles around again.

This is teamwork. This is taking each other seriously as thinking human beings. This is speaking the truth in love.

I wonder how the ongoing debate among evangelicals regarding gender would look if key leaders on various sides of this issue practiced this wisdom better than many seem to do. My impression is that most prominent speakers and authors on such matters talk right past their "opponents" to their respective cheering fans. They rarely seem to welcome the arguments of those who disagree with them as encounters with the concerns of fellow Christians, encounters that might lead to mutual edification.

Biblical feminists, it seems to me, are right to ask proponents of subordination or "complementarity" just why God would want women to be led by men in the home and the church, always and everywhere. Are men more intelligent or more spiritual and thus naturally better decision makers? Are men categorically superior leaders in other respects? The habit of subordinationists of simply invoking the "creation order" and other biblical passages, however appropriate this might be on some levels of this debate, does not answer these sensible questions. God seems to have good reasons for his instructions to us on other matters: Surely subordinationists ought to at least consider what they might be in this case.

Biblical feminists have some arguing to do as well. Just why would God have embedded egalitarianism so deeply in patriarchalism throughout the Bible? If, for example, God has always intended men and women to be equal and undifferentiated partners in home and church, as they are (at least ostensibly) in modern society, then why did God inspire such apparently contradictory and sweeping commands from Paul without qualification from any other New Testament authority—including Jesus? And given that most Christians have understood the Bible in a patriarchal mode for all these centuries, why did God not give the egalitarian key to this puzzle to any generation until our own?

I wonder when someone, somewhere, will promote the idea of holding a conference for evangelicals in North America that centers around just this procedure of sincere argument. Perhaps a Christian college or seminary or an organization such as the National Association of Evangelicals or InterVarsity Christian Fellowship could get the Christians for Biblical Equality and the Council for Biblical Manhood and Womanhood to nominate a handful of their chosen spokespeople. Then a real engagement over several days could ensue in which each of these two groups (and representatives of other positions as well) would simply have to keep listening and responding to each other, rather than preaching easily to their own choirs as they do year after year.

On another front, I wonder why certain theologians of a Reformed or Calvinist bent seem intent not just on blessing the rest of the evangelical community with the insights of their tradition but on castigating their fellow evangelicals on every point on which they differ from Reformed doctrine as interpreted by these theological vigilantes. Do they really think that other Christians disagree with them only because those Christians are either too stupid to see the obvious truth of Reformed theology or too stubborn to admit to its superiority? They might profitably consider the possibility that God has broken forth truth out of his Word that challenges the established categories of this single mode of Christian thought.

The same goes for advocates of the "Third Wave" of Christian spirituality, now washing over various parts of North America and elsewhere around the world. How much are they truly listening to the criticism of Christian brothers and sisters who do not want them to fail but rather to succeed in living as abundantly as possible?

I wonder when these champions of Reformed doctrine or Third Wave renewal will sponsor meetings to which they invite leading proponents of other points of view to an honest and earnest Christian discussion, rather than sponsoring yet more rallies of the already convinced. And perhaps a private conference, out of the media spotlight, would be a good place to start. Such privacy would minimize the temptation to play to the galleries and maximize the opportunity for true Christian fellowship even in theological disagreement.

We North American evangelicals have not handled the issues of inerrancy or creation science very well. Typically, we have been alarmed by the emergence of other points of view. We have not paused to investigate the issues thoroughly or to consider mediating positions. Instead, we have followed self-appointed leaders on crusades against all who disagree with us. We have mounted political campaigns of total war: removing dissidents from their jobs, taking over institutions that formerly housed more than one point of view and enforcing our own, and damning all those who resist our holy cause.

We have not stopped to listen, to consider, and to engage in mutually respectful argument. Our passionate commitments (to pro-life policies, to doctrinal truths, to spiritual vitality, to the family, to race and gender equality) tend to make us see everything as right or wrong, as "us" or "them." We are rightly afraid of a relativism that forbids anyone to claim possession of truth, but we overcompensate by allowing no room for self-doubt. We don't even pause for the self-examination that would result if we actually took the trouble to set our arguments in order. Instead, we have taken our convictions for granted as gospel truth. And when confronted by those who differ with us, we have just reached for the stick, confident that we already knew the truth, the whole truth, and nothing but the truth, so that all that remained was conquest of the enemy. Contrary to the biblical injunction (James 1:19), we think we don't need to listen. We love to speak, and boy, are we quick to get angry.

Yet only a fool resists good argument. Only a proud, self-satisfied person (or organization) resists a better idea when presented with one. The Proverbs of the Bible repeat over and over again that the wise person *delights* in correction and positively *seeks it out:* "A scoffer who is rebuked will only hate you; the wise, when rebuked, will love you. Give instruction to the wise, and they will become wiser still; teach the righteous and they will gain in learning" (Prov. 9:8–9). When we argue with each other in a biblical way—rather than simply shout at each other, insult each other, ignore each other, or scheme against each other—we honor each other as wise ones who desire to grow in wisdom.

These exhortations, furthermore, are applicable well beyond theological controversies. Sermons should not just *tell* us what the Bible says or refer to the Bible or have a vague connection with the Bible: They should *show* us that the Bible says what the preacher thinks it says. Verse-by-verse exposition is only one method of doing so. Every preacher, whatever his or her preaching style, ought to demonstrate to the congregation at every key point just how that point arises naturally from a fair-minded and obedient reading of Scripture. Otherwise, the congregation can have no clear idea that it is encountering the Word of God in a sermon rather than merely a concern, a word of advice, or a passing fancy of the preacher's own. I wonder about any preacher, frankly, whose sermons don't both inspire and *require* an audience to listen with Bibles open.

Congregational leaders should not just *tell* us that such-and-such an action is a good idea: They should *show* us that such-and-such is a good idea and then welcome improvements. How often in your church do the leaders (whether elders, deacons, or vestry) inform the congregation regularly of the issues they are *currently* discussing or are *going* to discuss and invite ideas and opinions? (They could do so in church bulletins, newsletters, and other announcements without much trouble.) How often do they call a church forum to solicit help from the collective wisdom of the gathered church?

Parents should not just *tell* children to do this or that: They should *show* their children that the parental instruction is right—as circumstances and the children's ages permit, of course. As a parent of three boys myself, I have found sometimes that when I explain why I want something done, it becomes clear that my motives are suspect. It is for my convenience, say, rather than for their benefit. Sometimes my sons can suggest a better way of proceeding. I might then be a little embarrassed, but we all win when such exchanges bear such good fruit. And if I happen to be proven correct in the end, then perhaps my sons will see that they are going ahead with my request not just because of sheer parental authority but because it is, after all, a good idea.

Public activists should not just *tell* fellow citizens what they think about something: They should *show* them why they think so. They should do so not by hurling the Bible at them (which usually has the same effect as a Mormon or a Muslim preaching at you from his or her own scriptures) but by coming alongside them and showing them, according even to their own principles, how problematic their views are and how much better others might be. Richard John Neuhaus, Cornel West, and Bill Bennett are Christian "arguers" who speak to the public in terms a wide audience can appreciate. We must speak the language of those we are trying to persuade—at least, we must do so as far as we can without compromising our Christian faith, as Paul did on the Areopagus. Frankly, our failure to do this may point to a lack in our empathy or our reasoning. Furthermore, perhaps we ourselves might learn something valuable in the process, including something of the common humanity of our political opponents.

Our families, churches, and society are fragmenting into sullen individuals and militant factions. One of the attitudes that is tearing us apart is the insistence that everyone else better just agree with me when I give my opinion—and if some refuse to do so, then I'll write them off and associate exclusively with those who will. As the T-shirts read when Nelson Mandela first visited New York City, "It's a black thing. You wouldn't understand." Buzz off: It's a female thing/it's a Baptist thing/it's a homosexual thing/it's a conservative thing. You wouldn't understand.

We badly need instead an attitude of Christian humility that affirms that we don't know it all and that we'd like to know more. We badly need an attitude of Christian appreciation that recognizes what other people can give us that we do not have ourselves. We badly need an attitude of Christian obedience to the truth and a sacrifice of the ego so that the question is always *what's* right, not *who's* right—to the glory of God.

And so, as a seeker of gracious, edifying discourse in our friendships, families, churches, and workplaces, I invoke the magisterial Pythons once again and cry, "I'd like to have an argument, please."

20

Hail to the Faithful!

Some Christians get a lot of recognition for what they do. Some write best-selling books. Others lead impressive organizations. Some accomplish dramatic feats, while others become popular entertainers.

Most Christians, however, do not get a lot of recognition for what they do. Yet they should. So let us raise a toast to the usually unsung faithful, the Christians who do most of the work while a minority gets most of the affirmation. Grab your glass of milk, your tumbler of juice, your goblet of wine, your stein of beer, your demitasse of tea, your mug of coffee, your bottle of soda pop—whatever your cup of cheer—and join with me in praising our fellow servants.

- Hail to the Sunday school teacher poring over her lesson plan after a long day's work, cutting out materials for the class, learning a new song to teach her students, considering yet another method for disciplining little Johnny, and praying for each of the children entrusted to her instruction every week.

- Hail to the organist shopping for new music, practicing by the hour alone in the sanctuary, and on Sunday playing a splendid postlude to the glory of God that no one else really listens to in the din of after-church conversation.
- Hail to the church accountant keeping track of the finances, running down errant invoices and receipts, praying over the budget and the offerings each month, and telling us the truth about our stewardship.
- Hail to the youth worker overwhelmed by the problems of his young charges, exhausted by another late-night event, running out of fresh ideas and yet providing a place of safety and fun and encouragement and instruction for our needy teens.
- Hail to the scholar alone in her study or library carrel, investing months or years to clarify the meaning of one Bible verse or the events of one historical episode, the structure of one sonnet or the nature of one chemical reaction. No one but other experts can appreciate this work, upon which all of our knowledge depends—no one else but God, who created the world and calls us to understand it, appreciate it, and steward it with the help of such expertise.
- Hail to the manager who creates pleasant and productive environments for her workers. Hail to the worker who gives a good day's work even for less than a good day's pay. And hail to the owner who cares more about providing useful goods and services than about maximizing profit.
- Hail to the homemaker desperate to get out of the house, drained of energy, confronted on every side with evidence that her family takes her for granted—hail her as she sits down on the floor to help her toddler with a puzzle one more time.
- Hail to those who pray—who pray a lot and pray well. Hail to those who have the ear of God and make the most of their privilege on behalf of others. Hail to the old people, the sick people, the quiet people, whose prayers support the rest of us, keeping us from drowning in filthy seas and enabling us to succeed in our work, whether we recognize their essential help or not.
- Hail to the altar guild member, the custodian, the snow shoveler, the groundskeeper, whose work reminds us (if we will stop to consider it) that God loves the body as well as the soul, that

God recognizes the material as well as the spiritual, and that God receives with approval and affection the offerings of each of these servants.

Yes, let us toast them all! Perhaps there are more we should recognize and whom you can recognize in the circle of your church fellowship. By doing so, let's give thanks to the Center of that circle, from whom all blessings flow.

21

Shaking Hands with a "Label"

Getting to know Helen was a disillusioning experience. I once worked on an academic committee with a professor from the women's studies department. I knew about feminists. I knew about women's studies. And I knew about homosexuals. Getting to know Helen, however, shattered the illusion that I knew all I should know about these three subjects.

Helen was a feminist, dedicated in her professional and personal life to bettering the lot of women in a society still tilted toward men. She was a rising star in her department. She was also, as she later told me, a lesbian who lived with her long-time female partner.

I found that Helen was an accomplished scholar and a dedicated teacher. She worked hard on academic committees to improve the life of the university. I found her to be a kind, thoughtful, and gentle person. In the helter-skelter of academic politics, she became one of my favorite colleagues. I think, and hope, that our friendship might have disconfirmed some of her unhappy stereotypes about evangelical

Christian men. I *know* that she disconfirmed some of *my* stereotypes about feminist lesbians teaching in women's studies.

Now here's the point. I continue to hold strong views about homosexuality, feminism, and women's studies. Getting to know and to like Helen didn't change those views very much. But it did have one very practical result: I never think of those issues and never speak or write about them without thinking of that real person, a person I enjoy and respect, who exemplifies them.

We tend to demonize those with whom we have strong disagreements. We know we're supposed to love our neighbors, but the urge is strong to view certain neighbors not as real people but only as symbols of things we dislike. "He is an assertive male, which reminds me of my abusive father, so I'll treat him as such." "She is mystically inclined, so I'll treat her as I would any flaky New Ager." "She is a teacher/pastor/manager, so I'll treat her as a tyrant, since I know that all authority figures are inclined that way."

How convenient. We can label people we meet according to the causes or the past injuries, sins, or follies that they represent to us. We can write a scarlet letter on her, an "idiot" sign on him (see Matt. 5:22), and be done with them.

Real acquaintance, however, changes things. We can no longer demonize "them," whoever "they" are, once we've actually met a member of that faceless set. Acquaintance shows us that he or she is not a demon but a human being. I wonder how much of our conversation, how much of our preaching, how much of our joking, and how much of our view of the world would change if we actually got to know someone in "their" camp, whatever that camp might be. I expect, at least, that there would be fewer flip comments about and fewer easy dismissals of "gays," "liberals," "charismatics," "feminists," "men," "Indians," "kids today," or "clergy" if we did so.

At the same time, such personal acquaintance reminds us of a complementary and quite sober truth: Even nice people can hold bad, even dreadful, opinions and behave in unhelpful, even destructive, ways. Including you. Including me.

Acquaintance doesn't always alter our convictions, nor should it. But it can change the way we treat each subject—as if real human beings were involved, *which they always are*. How much worse for us to conduct disputes *within* the Christian church as if those who disagree with us are not our brothers and sisters in Christ but the devil's minions whom we must simply and utterly oppose.

Don't we ourselves hope that our neighbors won't simply write us off once they know we are Christians because they have already made up their minds about everyone in that category? Don't we cringe to hear "evangelical" equated with bigotry, sexism, and stupidity?

Something about a Golden Rule comes to mind. . . .

22

Grunting Our Appreciation?

Dictionaries of slang tell us a lot about our culture. One could guess, for instance, that both getting drunk and having sex are significant for North Americans, given the wide array of expressions for each. Naturally, I shan't compromise the dignity of this sober volume by listing examples here. Doubtless the point is made sufficiently well by the synonyms already popping up in the mind of each reader.

We also, however, have developed a wide vocabulary to describe people we don't like. When someone annoys, offends, or injures us, we usually can go beyond a general term of contempt to nail him or her with a vivid characterization of the evil action and the evil perpetrator. Again, I shan't stoop to offer examples. Surely you're not such a bonehead that you can't think of at least a few by yourself.

When we encounter good actions and good people, however, many of us seem tongue-tied. We warmly, but weakly, pronounce that such-and-such was "really nice" and so-and-so is "a really good guy." Most of us have trouble giving compliments, and when we do, our words either immediately evanesce in their worn-out generality ("great/

neat/cool") or thunk to the ground in clumsiness ("Y'know, Clara-belle, you're just, um—well, you're just really pretty . . .").

Others of us are freer, more skilful. A journalist tells of sitting in on a meeting of Billy Graham and his inner circle of friends. One of them compliments another. The compliment is quickly returned and aug-mented. Others join in, and the kind words now bounce back and forth around the circle in a free-for-all badminton game of genuine praise. The journalist has never seen anything like it.

We speak disparagingly of a "mutual admiration society." But surely the Christian community is to be at least a "mutual *affirma-tion* society," as we mediate God's love to each other *in word* as well as in deed.

And those words need to multiply in variety and exactness, as well as in frequency. Some people, in writing or speech, have the skill to bestow compliments with poise and accuracy. The Bible itself describes its particular heroes in colorful precision and sets out shin-ing lists of the diverse qualities of the worthy person of God. Such terms and expressions merit our study and use.

There is a troubling question at the heart of this issue. The Inuit, so it is said, have many terms for different forms of snow. Snow is vital to them, so they have learned to observe and describe it carefully. Perhaps our impoverished vocabularies of praise signify just what about human beings we find important—literally "remarkable"—and what we in fact do not value so much. Why are our lexicons so rich in condemnation and so poor in praise?

Some Christians profess worry at this point about the terrible dan-ger of fostering pride. "Oh, dear," they fret, "we can't go on and on about people in case they become conceited." And there is a strand of hero worship and celebrity mongering in evangelicalism that ought indeed to be chastened. Perhaps, however, most of us have been rather too enthusiastic about this job of humbling each other—a task that properly belongs to *God*—and not energetic enough about our true calling of building each other up.

Such a community of sincere encouragement would stand out from a fickle culture that adores the superficial and suspects the noble. Per-haps our friends outside the church would more readily accept our invitation to come inside if there was life-giving warmth to be enjoyed.

The apostle exhorts us, "Love one another with mutual affection; outdo one another in showing honor" (Rom. 12:10). So let the blessed competition of compliments increase. Hit me with your best shot.

23

The Wo/men's Issue

Words don't mean everything, but they mean something. One of the follies and one of the insights of political correctness is its preoccupation with language: folly, because changing words doesn't automatically change the world; insight, because changing words can help change the world.

One change many Christians need to make has to do with the question of gender roles in church and home. As any good debater knows, the way in which one puts a question helps to restrict the kinds of answers that can be given. This issue is often discussed under the title "the women's issue" rather than under the term "gender," and from this usage a number of fallacious ideas can follow.

One might conclude, for instance, that only women care about this matter—it's only an "issue" for *them*. But many of us men care deeply about women's responsibilities and opportunities, and we work to improve them. Ironically, many women themselves *don't* see anything wrong with the situations they are in and don't see what all the fuss is about.

One might conclude, second, that this issue *affects* only women—it's a matter, one might think, of deciding how women ought to function in relation to the established positions of men. But so-called second-wave feminism sweeps past the first-wave conviction that women and men are interchangeable, unisex parts that can fit equally into this or that social structure—a structure, indeed, that usually has been constructed by men. This newer and more nuanced approach to gender suggests that women and men are in fact different and that as women play their appropriate parts in any society, the structures will in fact be altered according to women's viewpoints and preferences. Those alterations thus affect the roles of everyone, women and men both. The life of the whole body will be changed thereby.

Taken together, these two erroneous conclusions often lead to a third: that this is a question that can be safely, properly, and *indefinitely* deferred in the interests of church unity, in the interests of mission, in the interests of the gospel itself. After all, maybe some women in our congregation, denomination, or parachurch institution are upset about what they see as sexism. And maybe it's true that our organizations can make better use of some of these women. But let's not push things too dangerously far. Let's not allow too much challenge of the status quo. This debate is not about the gospel, you see: It's a secondary issue.

So many Christian women, and men, finally give up pressing for change in resistant congregations, denominations, and parachurch institutions, and they leave for more hopeful ones. The group thus fragments after all, and in doing so it loses energetic and gifted members. So other women, and men, enter our churches or other institutions and find that for all of the importance granted gender issues on the "outside," these Christian groups still refuse to take this matter seriously in open discussion and significant action. And evangelism thereby suffers.

No, gender controversy is not about the most elementary expression of the gospel. But when our understanding and practice of gender roles serve to weaken Christian groups and to repel inquirers, it becomes a gospel issue. And it becomes an issue for *all* of us. Thoughtful defenders of *various* views understand this reality, as they all see that changing, or not changing, the roles of women will affect fundamentally the roles of men and the overall structuring of home and church.

Are you a woman? Then this is an issue for you. Are you a man? Then this is an issue for you too. Are you involved in a Christian organization that involves both men and women? Then this is also an issue for you.

It's not "the women's issue." It's *our* issue. And it can't be deferred.

24

An Ounce of Prevention

Remi De Roo is a retired Canadian Roman Catholic bishop widely respected for his work on behalf of the poor. A short while ago, he confessed to financial mismanagement that led, with bitter irony, to the impoverishment of his former diocese on Vancouver Island.

Around the same time, Amy Grant, American star of Christian and secular pop music, announced the breakup of her marriage due to her love affair with another performer, country singer Vince Gill.

I remember the dark days of the two Jimmys, Swaggart and Bakker, as they disgraced themselves and the religion they preached when they were exposed in tawdry sins. I confess that at the time I felt a certain comfortable distance from these brothers. I disdained them, in fact, as so much "white trash" from whom such behavior might be expected by more sophisticated folk such as myself—until pastors Gordon MacDonald and Frank Tillapaugh, heroes of middle-class evangelicalism, confessed to sexual misconduct of their own.

It occurred to me then, and I'd like to pass this on to you now, that we need to pray for our leaders every day that God will lead them not into temptation but deliver them from evil. We should, that is, pray for them *before* they get into trouble and pray that they *won't* get into trouble.

All of us, of course, need such prayer—not just leaders. That's why Jesus told his disciples to pray this way all the time. But those who symbolize our religion and direct us in our faith need special prayer support, for the breadth of their influence means greater blessing when they succeed and greater harm when they fail.

Let's not assume that those who currently ride high in Christian esteem are somehow immune to the sins that beset the rest of us. Indeed, it is often true in spiritual matters that the bigger they are, the harder they fall. The personality traits that help people succeed in such professions and ministries can also leave them vulnerable to pride, avarice, lust, greed—and the rest of the deadly sins.

The New Testament records that the apostle Paul himself asked several of his churches to pray for him, as did the inspired writer to the Hebrews. If they recognized that they needed prayer, who of us doesn't need it?

So when I read about Remi De Roo and Amy Grant, I prayed for them, for those hurt by their mistakes, and for those who were left to pick up the pieces. But years ago when I read about MacDonald, Tillapaugh, and the rest, I resolved to pray for a half dozen leaders who had *not* yet fallen—a few Canadians and a few Americans, each of whom has blessed me in some way. I have prayed regularly for them ever since.

I have prayed that they would remain morally upright. I have prayed that they would care properly for their families. I have prayed that they would wisely discern just how God would have them use their gifts best. And I have prayed that they would enjoy walking with God more and more.

No one has an easy life. No one is spiritually safe, outside the ever-lasting arms of God.

So perhaps today the Holy Spirit—who loves to prompt Christians to pray—will help you "adopt" a few prominent Christians to support in prayer. It might be the pastor of your own church. It might be a local writer, speaker, or singer. It might be a nationally or internationally renowned Christian whose work has especially impressed you.

Again, we mustn't neglect the prayers we should render for our neighbors, for those near to us who are our special responsibility. Prominent people don't count any more in the kingdom than anyone else. But let us not neglect them either, as they surely are strategically important targets for the evil one's missiles.

Whose ministry are you glad for? Then protect it, and protect him or her, in prayer.

PART 5

CHRISTIAN EDUCATION

25

Throw the Book at Them

ere's some copy from an actual toy advertisement in a major newsmagazine:

He's only 9. And yet he's thrown more touchdowns than John Elway, struck out more batters than Tom Clemens, birdied more holes than Tiger Woods, scored more goals than Wayne Gretzky, driven more laps than Jeff Gordon, and flown more missions than Luke Skywalker. He's rescued a dozen princesses, defended every planet from aliens, and landed choppers in hostile territory with full artillery blazing. What are you going to throw at him next?

Well, I must harrumph, how about a *book?* You know, those old-fashioned things with covers and pages and type and (dare I say it) actual *ideas?* Those static, just-sitting-there-quietly treasure chests of the imagination?

Nahhh. Everybody knows books are dull. And even worse, they require effort: effort to select in a bookstore or library, effort to read and understand. Bring on the Nintendo, the cartoons, the DVDs.

The late Allan Bloom, who taught at such universities as Yale, Paris, Chicago, and Toronto, lamented the intellectual state of young people when he encountered them as undergraduates. "When I first noticed the decline in reading during the late sixties," he testified, "I began asking my large introductory classes, and any other group of younger students to which I spoke, what books really count for them. Most are silent, puzzled by the question. The notion of books as companions is foreign to them." Instead, he wrote, they "turn to the movies."

Neil Postman of New York University decries our slide from a literate culture into an age of show business in which we spend our time, as his book title claims, *Amusing Ourselves to Death*. We no longer read, or at least we no longer read serious literature seriously. So we do not regularly follow plotlines and arguments for dozens of pages. So we do not think connectedly. And so we end up not really thinking at all.

Ah, you say. But Christians are "Bible people." We read at least *that* text regularly and seriously. We teach our children Bible stories, commit Scripture to memory, and engage in regular Bible study at home and church. Sure we do.

Not according to the poll data that show that 10 percent or fewer Canadians read the Bible even once a week, and the numbers are only somewhat higher in the United States. Not according to many evangelical observers who have remarked on the vanishing of the Bible in the many churches they visit: Few congregants bring their own, and not many use the pew Bibles during worship.

What other Christian literature we do read isn't impressively substantial. Check out the shelves and sales figures of Christian bookstores to see how we prefer spiritual milk to "strong meat."

My parents helped me to read—and to keep reading for a lifetime—in two key ways. My mother faithfully read to us children and patiently taught us to read. Then she wore a track on the road from our house to the public library. For his part, my father stamped an indelible image in my mind of a surgeon retiring to his study at the end of the day to sit in a pool of light and read. And in the late 1960s and early 1970s, as I recall, he wasn't reading medical manuals or pulp fiction. He was reading Paul Little, C. S. Lewis, and Francis Schaeffer. My mother enabled; my father exampled.

We are citizens of a highly complex culture who have the opportunity to participate in a wide range of decisions if only we know enough about them to form a responsible Christian opinion. Without disciplined, regular reading of thoughtful journals and books, however, we will have to defer to others who do understand and do know how to act effectively.

We may not, however, like where they lead us. Without reading, we and our children are sheep for the shearing, and perhaps for the slaughter, rather than well-prepared agents for God's kingdom.

The toy advertisement I quoted appeared on the back cover. The front cover of the magazine showed a TV screen and the headline "Prime-Time Violence."

What are we going to throw at the kids next, indeed?

26

If Your People Aren't Reading, Is It TV's Fault?

Why Don't Christians Read?

The top three reasons why Christians don't read: TV, TV, and TV.

The oft-cited figures say that the television is on more than seven hours a day in the average American home. Given the often forbidding Canadian climate, it is likely that we watch at least as much up here! Scott Stossel, writing in the *Atlantic Monthly*, says, "[TV] has become a member of the family, telling its stories patiently, compellingly, untiringly."

Yet because of the tremendous costs of producing television at "industry standard," the stories TV tells are controlled by a few powerful corporations: media empires and their advertising clients. And those stories, those windows on the world, have been shown in study after study to be both immoral and untrue to reality. TV does not show us typical families, typical religions, typical problems, and typical struggles. It shows us stereotypes instead, stereotypes that inhabit the fantasies of network, advertising, and other corporate executives and that are packaged by so-called creative elites in New York and Los Angeles.

How about saying, "Just turn it off"? George Gerbner, dean emeritus of the Annenberg School of Communication at the University of Pennsylvania, thinks such advice is an upper-middle-class conceit: "In most homes there is nothing as compelling as television at any time of the day or night."

I suggest to you, as one who himself watches several hours of TV every week (we tape favorite programs and watch them regularly), that Christian intellectual leaders—and pastors and Sunday school teachers especially—need to confront the phenomenon of TV more regularly, more directly, and more critically than they do.

Gerbner again: "Whoever tells most of the stories to most of the people most of the time has effectively assumed the cultural role of parent and school, . . . teaching us most of what we know in common about life and society." Stossel continues: "Television . . . has become a cultural force equaled in history only by organized religion. Only religion has had this power to transmit the same messages about reality to every social group, creating a common culture."

Television—not the church, not the Bible, not the government, not the schools, not literature, not newspapers—is telling the stories to most of the people most of the time.

If your people aren't reading, then yes, it's largely television's fault. And what they're getting from TV is probably pretty scary.

They Do Read, but What?

So if everyone is watching television, why are big box bookstores springing up everywhere? Why are there more books being printed than ever, more book sales than ever? You can't tell Stephen King, Danielle Steele, John Grisham, Michael Crichton, or a number of other best-selling novelists that people aren't reading.

You can't even tell that to Frank Peretti, Grant Jeffrey, Philip Yancey, or Janette Oke. You can't tell that to Christian Book Distributors, which has grown from a business in a garage to a multimillion-dollar sales industry in less than twenty years, or to the Christian Booksellers Association, one of the fastest sectors of growth in the publishing industry over the same period. And *somebody* is reading millions of copies of Left Behind fiction.

Some people, therefore, maybe more than you or I might have thought, are indeed reading. But what? Are they reading the best fiction, the best theology, the best advice, the best stuff available?

How can they do so without guidance? Consider now your own people, the people you serve and who look to you for Christian leadership. How are they supposed to find out about the best book, or even a good book, to read on a given subject?

Bookstores, no matter how well organized, are still bewildering places for many people. How are they to work through a shelf of books on a subject that interests them? What clues can they use to determine whether this book or that book is more likely to meet their needs? Who is going to teach them how to pick good books and how to read them well?

The staff at most Christian bookstores do not know serious Christian books well. They probably know pop music and gifts much better. And secular bookstores are, predictably, hopeless when it comes to religious reading. Someone else, therefore, needs to help your people know what to look for in those stores.

Another major problem, however, is that even if you can persuade people to read, or read more, or read better, the actual books need to be available. Not many people want to use mail order, and e-business has not taken off the way some predicted it would. Not many people like to special order in a store. Ideally, books are in stock somewhere in the city in a bookstore or library that people enjoy visiting. Yet secular bookstores stock few worthy titles in their "religion sections." University bookstores aren't much better. And Christian bookstores seem to major on fluff, polemics, and self-help—if you can find the books at all, behind the music, videos, and gifts for sale.

What to Do?

First, encourage and equip your people to read.

- Tell them to turn off the TV and read. Tell them why TV is harmful. (Read some Neil Postman or George Gerbner if you're not sure, especially Postman's *Amusing Ourselves to Death: Public Discourse in an Age of Show Business.*) Turn off the TV news and spend fifteen minutes instead gathering news from a daily newspaper, weekly newsmagazine, or news web site. Then spend the other fifteen minutes on a book.

Someone who undertakes this discipline will be better informed about current events (because they will learn much more in the same time—we can read faster than we can "watch") and also will read—using just an extra fifteen minutes per day—another dozen books a year.

- Show that you read by mentioning and recommending books from the pulpit or lectern and in every other context you can.
- Teach good reading skills in adult Christian education. Perhaps there is a teacher in your congregation skilled in this particular kind of instruction, or perhaps you can bring in someone for a seminar. It is hard to think of many skills more valuable than reading skills for Christians in our culture.

Next, form an alliance with a Christian bookstore. Ideally, there should be two-way communication and cooperation between you and a local Christian store.

- You should be able to tell such a store that you frequently recommend the following half dozen titles, and you'd like to be sure that a local store will have them in stock when you do recommend them. If you're planning a sermon or lesson series on a particular area, inform the bookstore about your topic in advance so they can order relevant books.
- You should be able to say to someone, "I don't know of a good book in that area, but visit Bookstore X and see what they have. They usually have a good range of things, and they try to stock only good quality books." For its part, the bookstore should help you keep abreast of what is new and welcome your suggestions whenever you offer them.
- The bookstore should be able to count on regular referrals from you. It should also be able to count you among its customers, as another Christian willing to put his money where his mouth

is in support of this service. I'm not saying you should just hand over your money to the bookstore as if it's a charity. It's not. It's a business. But we sometimes forget that if we don't patronize local businesses and instead send our dollars to discount houses or specialty bookstores elsewhere, those local businesses will not be able to afford to stock books we like (since people like us always shop elsewhere)—if they can afford to stay in business at all.

Pastors, other ministry professionals, and bookstore owners are all gatekeepers. You decide which books to tout and which books to ignore, and in so doing you shape the reading habits of the people you lead. Indeed, you reveal whether good reading is a priority for Christians both by what you say and by what you don't say.

Pastors in some traditions used to be called "parsons," the "important person." The origins and uses of this term are various, but one meaning is "the cultural and intellectual leader of the flock." I am sorry to lay a burden on your already well-laden shoulders, but I'm afraid you may have to take up this role once again!

Yet try to see the encouragement of reading as a way of extending and even lightening your ministry. (Educators do this all the time with textbooks and other assigned reading.) If your people are reading, they can learn more than you can say. They can learn it from others rather than yourself. And all of this can complement what you are trying to do for them and with them. Your ministry thereby multiplies.

And may I observe in closing, all of this effort might also produce an additional benefit: Perhaps they'll watch less TV.

27

Reading on Purpose

Why read? It may seem absurd to begin an essay in a book with this question. Isn't anyone who's reading this page already convinced that reading is a good thing?

The question here, however, is more particular. Just why are you reading this—or anything else? Effective reading is directed reading. The best reading is done "on purpose," with clear goals in mind.

We read for ideas: practical ideas to help us with a specific challenge and theoretical ideas to help us understand an issue. We read to encounter difference, to consider alternatives to what we take for granted. We read to enjoy the play of language, the power and beauty of skillfully wrought prose and poetry—and to strengthen, sharpen, and quicken our own skills. And we read to make new friends among authors ancient and modern who live in their books and offer us themselves as often as we wish to consult them.

A special word about fiction might balance the Christian tendency to relegate it to the "leisure" category only. Certain kinds and qualities of fiction are entryways into human experience that call us to attention with vividness and power. As Flannery O'Connor puts it, "The beginning of human knowledge is through the senses, and the fiction writer begins where human perception begins. He appeals through the senses, and you cannot appeal to the senses with abstractions. . . . The first and most obvious characteristic of fiction is that it deals with reality through what can be seen, heard, smelt, tasted, and touched."

Theologian Cornelius Plantinga challenges preachers explicitly, and the rest of us implicitly, to read fiction "for character." As he writes, "Few of us have experience rich and vast enough and few of us are observant enough to furnish ourselves with a full knowledge of character drawn just from direct observation." Instead, we must gain it vicariously through fiction—and history too. "To a preacher," he concludes, and to the rest of us as well, "reading for character is not merely an option. If you are going to talk about people, you have to know them."

Why read, however, instead of watching or listening to broadcast media? One reads because one can control better (if not absolutely) what one encounters. Print lets one scan the headlines or a table of contents and pick stories to consider out of a newspaper or select chapters in a book. One can also control the display. One can slow down a passage or go over it again, or even stop completely and stare off into space to ponder it at length. With this control and this consideration comes the opportunity for a kind of conversation with the writing, a chance to respond—even in pausing to write out one's own reflections.

If we're going to read, then, as Christian disciples we must consider how to engage in disciplined reading. Given each of our various callings, blanket recommendations that everyone ought to read this book or that periodical make little sense. But what too few of us do is make a consistent effort to read the *best* version of whatever we read.

Consider how many books and magazines you read in an average month. Then calculate your average annual reading and multiply it by the time you have left in an average life span. For most of us, that will amount to a pretty small shelf. So how can we justify spending time on mediocre reading when there's good reading to be had? How can we read good material instead of the best?

We find out about the best by regularly scanning the book review pages of the best quality magazines in our areas of interest and then filing items away for future purchase or borrowing. We ask knowledgeable acquaintances to recommend titles, and we invariably find them delighted to help. We also develop the habit of reading even carefully selected literature with a critical eye: If this section or this chapter isn't of sufficient relevance or quality, we skip it and move on. (Some of us neurotically feel that we're somehow "quitting" if we stop reading a book before the end—as if books we've read are trophies on our shelves! No, they are merely artifacts to be enjoyed and then set aside when no longer useful to us.)

We also learn to think about books or articles as products of particular minds rather than as self-contained entities. That is, as we grow in our reading sophistication, we begin to notice and then to remember the names of particular authors, and we rejoice in new authorial friends while we deepen our relationships with old acquaintances.

Those old acquaintances—or new friends—might really be old. It is a badly restricted reading diet that is limited to contemporaries. How rich is the fare offered by the great works of Augustine, Julian of Norwich, Martin Luther, John Milton, John Bunyan, Blaise Pascal, and Gerard Manley Hopkins! And beyond the Christian heritage lie many more treasures for the determined seeker. C. S. Lewis once recommended his discipline of reading at least one "old" book for every "new" one, but some of us need to *start* with one "old" one!

Once we are reading something worthy, we must engage it in critical conversation. Mortimer Adler and Charles Van Doren instruct us in such interaction in their enduringly useful *How to Read a Book*. Evangelical author James Sire complemented this with his own guide *How to Read Slowly*. We know how to read, but many of us probably don't read very *well*.

Researchers of reading (there are such people) tell us that we tend to read everything at more or less the same speed. Instead, we should purposefully speed over items that we can understand easily or that we don't need to understand thoroughly and then slow down over material that demands tenacious concentration. We passively sit and soak rather than actively listen, question, and respond. One wise person has said that we must never read a book without entering in the margin at least one yes and one no. Indeed, to profit fully from serious reading we must articulate our responses more clearly, perhaps in writing full sentences in top and bottom margins or extended entries in a blank book or journal.

Yet who has time to read? Well, people who watch TV can turn it off and read. People who can forego fifteen minutes of sleep and read in the evening or early morning can read an extra book or two a month. People who decide that the ongoing development of their minds will be of some good to their spouses, their children, their friends, their clients, and their God will make time to read.

Some will have to find a refuge in which to read, a place of peace outside the bustle of their normal environment. Some will escape the phone and hide in libraries, those glorious sanctuaries dedicated to the splendid possibilities of literature. Others will retreat into bathrooms and bedrooms. Still others will prop a reading stand on the exercise bike standing dusty in the basement and blow the cobwebs off their brains as well.

But some of us will come out of the closet and boldly read in the living room right in front of spouse and children, right in front of roommates, prizing reading no matter what surprise and derision it might elicit from one's significant others. Indeed, once their shock subsides, they might just settle down and read too.

So let's read often, read well, and read heartily to the Lord, who commanded us to love God with our minds.

28

Just Two Is Just Fine

once accepted an invitation to teach a summer school course at a Canadian theological seminary. It was July 1990, and I offered a course on "Canadian Evangelicalism" in the evenings for two weeks. Given this seminary's location in a major Canadian city and the pertinence of this course to its constituency, I looked forward to a large audience.

Precisely three students enrolled. And one of them dropped the course halfway through. Each evening for a fortnight, then, I faithfully showed up and taught the students, both of whom faithfully attended class and completed their assignments. Yet often, I confess, it was difficult for me to stay motivated to teach just two students.

In a recent autobiographical sketch (in the fine collection of Kelly Clark's *Philosophers Who Believe*), Yale University philosopher Nicholas Wolterstorff recalls his student days at Calvin College in Michigan. Once, he writes, he signed up for a course on Immanuel Kant's difficult *Critique of Pure Reason*. Taught by a distinguished professor, Harry Jellema, the course enrolled just two students.

Nicholas Wolterstorff was one. Alvin Plantinga, now professor of philosophy at Notre Dame University, was the other. Wolterstorff delightedly notes that every student in that class has since been invited to give the prestigious Gifford Lectures in Scotland, defending the Christian faith. Today Wolterstorff and Plantinga are unquestionably two of the leading Christian philosophers in the world. And they look back on Jellema's class as a seminal experience in their development as philosophers. Jellema, though, could not have foreseen any of that when he faithfully entered his classroom each time to teach just these two students.

At the University of Chicago, students still enjoy telling the story of astrophysics professor Subrahmanyan Chandrasekhar. In the 1950s, Chandrasekhar was living in Wisconsin but was conducting research at the university's observatory. The university scheduled him to teach one advanced seminar that winter, so Chandrasekhar drove eighty miles each way to teach the course to—you guessed it—just two students. He could have canceled it, but he did not.

In the subsequent decades, both of those students, and Professor Chandrasekhar himself, won Nobel Prizes. Chandrasekhar, however, could not have foreseen any of that when he faithfully entered that classroom every time to teach just two students.

How can we escape the constant temptation to equate magnitude with importance? Length of resumé, size of congregation, cost of house, number of friends, list of commitments: Too small? Too bad.

But maybe *two* is enough, if it is God's will done in God's way. Who knows what our investment in one, or two, or six, or ten people will yield—in a friendship, in a Sunday school class, in job training, in coaching? Who knows what will happen when two or three are gathered together, or when just twelve are selected for a particular task?

I thought about all of this one August as I prepared to teach my own classes at the University of Manitoba. The introductory classes were always full, so I could count on large audiences in those. But I could see on the dean's printout that my advanced seminar in religion and philosophy would be attended by just two students.

I could hardly wait.

PART 6

REVIVAL/
RENEWAL

29

Background to Blessing

Not long ago, the power of God fell on a Canadian congregation. Hundreds of men and women of all sorts were so powerfully moved by preaching and prayers that they wept, laughed, trembled, roared, and collapsed, "slain in the Spirit." Some converted to Christianity; others returned to the faith they had forsaken; many more were strengthened in the faith they already had.

Some time later, the showers of blessing descended again. People came from near and far to experience healing, exorcism, speaking in tongues, and exhortation to holy living while all around them men and women swayed and shook, many falling to the ground. Pastors of several denominations came to witness the events, and, said one observer, "Many are going away never to be the same again."

These instances, however, are not chapters from the recent stories of the "Toronto Blessing" or the "Brownsville Miracle." The first account was of the "Canada Fire" burning at the Hay Bay camp meeting near Kingston, Ontario, in 1805. The second was of the "Latter Rain" falling in North Battleford, Saskatchewan, in 1948. These are instances of phenomena that have appeared in church history time and again throughout the world.

Also not new are the controversy and extremism that such revivals tend to foster. Then as now, congregations are riven as each party insists that all Christians ought to experience God in the way its members have done so. The enthusiasts claim superiority for their new way (a way that is new to *them*); traditionalists claim the high ground for themselves as defenders of the "old paths"; many in the middle are alienated from both extremes and so benefit little from either.

The colonial American pastor Jonathan Edwards participated in the Great Awakening that ignited much of eighteenth-century New England and settlements farther south. Edwards was a workaday pastor and thanked God for revival when it came to his own church, as it did to the churches of nearby towns. But he was also a brilliant scholar and brought his impressive intellectual talents to bear upon the crucial question that upset the entire culture: Were these extraordinary phenomena prompted by God, by sheer human enthusiasm, or by the devil?

In an early work, forged in the heat of controversy and commotion, Edwards set out ideas that he would later refine into the masterful *Treatise Concerning the Religious Affections* (now recognized as a classic in this subject). Edwards first listed nine different features of the revival of his day that he called "no-signs"—that is, features that could not point definitively to a positive or a negative source for the revival. Genuine renewal movements in the past had demonstrated some or all of these signs, he asserted, but so had clearly spurious ones. It was therefore a mistake for either critics or proponents of the revival to focus attention on these ambiguous qualities.

The nine "no-signs" briefly listed are as follows: (1) The work is carried on in an unusual way; (2) it produces strong effects on the bodies of participants; (3) it prompts a great deal of attention (Edwards called it "noise"!); (4) it stirs people's imaginations; (5) it is promoted too much by the influence of example and testimony; (6) it results in imprudent conduct; (7) errors in judgment and even "delusions of Satan" are intermingled with it; (8) some of its professed converts later fall into scandal; and (9) its preachers insist too much on the terrors of God's wrath.

Instead, Edwards affirmed, there are five luminous signs that a revival is truly of God: (1) It raises people's esteem of Jesus as Son of

God and Savior of the world; (2) it leads them to turn away from sin and toward holiness; (3) it increases their love for the Bible; (4) it grounds them in the basic truths of the faith; and (5) it evokes greater love for and service to God and other people.

Equipped with these guidelines, Edwards could allow that some people in the revival were being carried away by excess, others were immature, and still others perhaps were exploiting the situation for selfish ends. Still, he concluded, the awakening was essentially what he called a "surprising work of God," bearing authentic fruit immediately and promising still more in the future.

What is striking about Edwards's view is how much it echoes the wisdom of Christian mystics through the ages. Over and over, such spiritual adepts warn us that the passing moments of dramatic feeling are not to be clung to as the "normal Christian life" and certainly are not to be sought as ends in themselves. Instead, these mountaintop experiences are welcome places along the path of pilgrimage and service, happy punctuations of the routine of discipleship. So, too, the notorious barking and shaking and laughing and falling down are technically mere *epiphenomena,* only appearances on the surface of the *phenomena* that ultimately matter, the characteristics of maturing life in Christ. Thus, to indulge in controversy over the legitimacy of the spectacular epiphenomena is to miss the point: Is the church growing up in this revival or not?

The case of Pentecostalism, now over one hundred years old as a movement, demonstrates certain common dynamics of revival. Through the years it has generated considerable controversy, even as its proponents today are numbered around the globe. It has divided churches, but it has also refreshed others and started many new ones as well. Over time, furthermore, it has also cooled. Many North American Pentecostal meetings today are virtually indistinguishable from a Baptist service. From the clothes people wear to the music they sing, from the decor of the church to the demeanor of the pastor, it is clear that much of the fire that made Pentecostalism both attractive to some and repellent to others has disappeared. The same is true of the formerly spectacular Salvation Army, which a little over a century ago scandalized "proper" citizens with its outrageous brass bands and holy cartwheels.

It is also true that the impressive numerical gains of the earlier decades of these groups are now repeated only among immigrant populations in North America or in countries overseas. Otherwise, as recent studies have shown, Pentecostal growth in North America is quite moderate and no different from that of several other vital evangelical denominations.

Does this mean that Pentecostalism and the Salvation Army have matured beyond their youthful excesses? Does this mean instead that they have lost their original, authentic passion? What it means, at least, is that revivals have never burned "white hot" for long. The extraordinary camp meetings of the nineteenth century in the United States and Canada evolved into the properly maintained and predictably scheduled summer camps of the twentieth. Institutions, like individuals, cannot persist in a state of high excitement when much of what the world needs and God requires is day-by-day faithfulness: long-distance hiking, not straight-track sprinting.

Mention of Pentecostalism brings a historical irony to the surface. Just as the Toronto Blessing seems to have picked up the torch from moderate Pentecostalism, the Azusa Street Mission in Los Angeles emerged out of a cooling Holiness movement, going on to ignite international Pentecostalism. The Holiness movement, in turn, had sought in the nineteenth century to bring renewed vigor to an increasingly moribund and "respectable" Methodism. And Methodism had begun in the eighteenth century as an attempt to enthuse a complacent Church of England.

This pedigree also suggests that while a later movement might see itself as more zealous than an earlier one, it must guard against feelings of spiritual superiority toward its forebears, for it is evident that Pentecostals, Holiness believers, Methodists, and Anglicans all have continued to worship, believe, love, and serve God faithfully through the years. The new excitement in town might now be at the Vineyard or some other "full gospel" church. But if history takes its usual turn, in due course this flood of blessing will eventually cut channels—channels that will reduce the spectacle, yes, but also, by God's grace, will direct the water of life where it is needed most.

30

Everybody Wants Revival and Renewal—Don't We?

evival and *renewal* are hopeful, powerful words that resonate down the corridors of Christian history and within the hearts of believers today. Such evocative words, though, mean different things to different people. And for some they are not hopeful at all but threatening.

What Is Revival?

Literally, of course, *revival* means "to live again." Less dramatically, it means to come back to strength from a weakened condition. The stereotypes of religious revivalism, however, come from nineteenth-century Canada and America. Rural camp meetings under canvas and trees later moved into the cities and became urban rallies with a common recipe: enthusiastic, even boisterous, singing;

long meetings repeated over a number of days; vivid, direct, and often indelicate preaching by itinerant revivalists sounding a clear call to individual decision; and the electric testimonies of the repentant. All of these combined into what at times was an explosive mix.

Strictly speaking, revival can come only to those already alive, and so it means simply stirring up the already converted to new spiritual vigor. Revivalists have known, however, that they encounter many who are churched but not born again, as well as those who are neither churched nor saved, and so they have blended the call to the converted with the call *to be* converted.

Revivalism made a deep impression on a number of evangelical traditions in North America. It became a popular, even regular, activity of churches and denominations. In some cases, the rustic summer camp meetings became comfortable summer campgrounds—with a few featuring fully equipped winterized homes. In others, churches held annual revival weeks, with the obligatory guest speaker and standard hopes for a spiritual lift. Revival became ritual, and many young people raised in such traditions have committed their lives to Christ "on schedule" during such "high days" in the evangelical church calendar.

What Is Renewal?

Revival and *renewal* are often used interchangeably, but one might discern different shades of meaning. Revival can be seen as focusing on the spiritual and the individual, with the changes thus wrought then blossoming at times to affect other dimensions of life. Renewal, on the other hand, is more deliberately reconstructive. Something in Christian *corporate* life needs to change. If revival is concerned with "new vitality," renewal is concerned especially with "new forms."

Medieval renewal movements, such as those of the Benedictines, Cistercians, and Franciscans, for example, revised the rules by which clergy lived in order to restore what adherents believed to be the "apostolic ideal" of discipleship. These believers struck new balances of work and worship and imposed new strictures on poverty, chastity, and obedience so as to bring freshness to a stale situation. The German Pietists of the eighteenth century, for another example, reordered Lutheran life so as to foster more intelligent, more active, and especially more heartfelt Christianity. They organized small-group fellowships; founded schools, orphanages, and other institutions; and revised both corporate and individual worship.

In our own time, renewal has been associated with at least two quite different phenomena. First, there have been the renewal fellowships within pluralized, "mainline" Protestant denominations, such as Methodist (in Canada, United), Anglican/Episcopalian, and Presbyterian. A particular issue, such as the ordination of women or of homosexuals, typically galvanizes such groups. They see such issues as the last, intolerable step in a long-standing deviation of their church from some earlier path of correctness and health. Thus, such groups normally concentrate on the particular issue at hand, but they do so as part of a broader struggle to revitalize their church in other respects as well.

The other kind of renewal is the charismatic sort. Beginning in the 1940s and 1950s with leaders such as preacher Oral Roberts and Demos Shakarian of the Full Gospel Business Men's Fellowship International, the charismatic movement crested in the 1960s and 1970s, especially in the Roman Catholic and Anglican communions. In the 1980s and 1990s, a wide range of churches also encountered the Vineyard movement, the prophecy movement, and other outbreaks of charismatic interest.

In each case of renewal, however, different structures, not just different passions, are high on the agenda. The renewal wine demands new institutional wineskins. However restricted the initial focus might be to this issue or that concern, renewal movements typically go on to challenge the very forms of the churches and other institutions they affect. Small groups form; healing and prophecy meetings are held; new leaders emerge; different music and liturgy styles are embraced; and relationships with Christians of like disposition but different denomination often develop.

What Is an Awakening?

Occasionally, the spiritual and structural impetus of a new movement sweeps beyond the lives of individuals, congregations, and even denominations. Sometimes the very nature of society is changed under the press of religious revitalization. This happened in the eighteenth century under the Wesleys and George Whitefield in England, under Whitefield and Jonathan Edwards in the American colonies, and under Henry Alline and others in the Canadian Maritimes. Such "awakenings" not only brought new life to thousands of individuals and scores of churches but actually reshaped the societies around them for a generation or more.

Historians debate the actual effects of such large-scale events. Did the Methodist awakening actually "salt" England against the extremes of the French Revolution and help produce the slowly liberalizing society of nineteenth-century Britain? Did the Great Awakening in America prepare the way for the American Revolution? Did the Great Awakening in the Maritimes keep Nova Scotia *out* of the Revolution to the south and instead help foster a more conservative but charitable and tolerant society in the eastern Canadian colonies? Whatever the answers, the fact of the questions indicates the grand scope of such events: religious at heart but wide in their influence.

American historian William McLoughlin puts it well in his classic study, *Revivals, Awakenings, and Reform:* "Revivals alter the lives of individuals; awakenings alter the world view of a whole people or culture." In this sense, Canadians and Americans have enjoyed many revivals, a variety of renewal movements, but few true awakenings.

Revival and Renewal as Threat

Many conservative churches and leaders approve of revival—as long as it is the formulaic, automatic sort that boosts attendance, giving, and enthusiasm for a week or so each year. But Christians who seek more abundant showers of blessing often meet with frustrating resistance from entrenched authorities.

It is in the very nature of revival and renewal (R/R), though, to threaten the status quo and those most privileged in and supportive of that situation. R/R obviously pronounces judgment on things as they are and declares that things need to change. R/R furthermore is unpredictable and risky: We know what we have now and we're used to it, but who knows what we will encounter tomorrow, next week, or next year if this impulse for change is given full rein?

Those who wish to further R/R in their churches—or parachurch organizations, for that matter—need to take some basic sociology into account. Stable institutions resist change, and those who prize both stability per se and the particular status quo of the institution, *and especially those who have been promoted to positions of authority in it,* naturally have deep vested interest in maintaining things as they are.

The reality, therefore, is that true agents for change almost never come from the center of such groups but from the periphery. White, middle-aged men of a certain education and outlook dominate most churches, so the impetus for change most likely will come either from other such men who cannot get into positions of power or, more likely, from those who are *not* white, middle-aged men: racial minorities, youth, women, seniors, and those of distinctly more or less education or social standing than those in the center.

This reality has generally characterized R/R movements in the past. Younger men and women of various ages have been prominent in such movements. R/R initiators often have had significantly more, or significantly less, education than the official leaders. Laypeople have been conspicuously active. Less often, people of other races have figured importantly. The irony is that churches that want new things to happen typically look to their established leaders to provide it, and they are—from a sociological point of view—precisely the *least* likely group to initiate any significant and lasting change in the status quo.

This helps to explain the "bend but don't break" response of some church people to an agenda of change. A little revival, a little freshness within the established order, can be tolerated and even welcomed. But any disruption of the defining ways and means of the group will be stoutly resisted. Only churches that actively seek leadership from the periphery as well as from the center will, therefore, experience any substantial R/R.

There is a threat to the other side as well, however. Historian and charismatic apologist Richard Riss in his *Survey of Twentieth-Century Revival Movements in North America* warns proponents of R/R that "there will be temptations to spiritual pride. . . . Various groups and individuals will become convinced that they alone are instrumental in the accomplishment of God's purposes." Opposition can provoke self-righteousness, and as a result, the campaign for R/R can produce precisely the opposite outcome.

Reformed and Always Reforming

Implicit in the ideal of R/R is a return to a lost condition, a "re-vival" or "re-newal." It may be a return simply to one's "first love"; it may be a wholesale return to the structures as well as the ideals of an earlier stage of church history. Whatever the scope of the change, the ideal of R/R is intrinsically revolutionary and revisionist.

Another irony, however, appears often in the history of R/R movements. Once a new form appears, it becomes the new norm and slowly hardens into place. Ritualistic "revivals" later may bring the occasional surge of new enthusiasm, but the pattern is set for the next generation or more. Only another genuinely revolutionary revival will offer significant vitality to such a situation.

The history of R/R shows that movements intent on bringing new life to a group—even a group with a heritage of R/R—often prompt schism instead. The new wine splits the old wineskins, and new wineskins must develop: Methodism out of the Church of England, Holiness movements out of Methodism, and Pentecostalism out of Holiness—this genealogy constitutes just one such line of descent.

One of the lesser known slogans of the Protestant Reformation sets out an alternative model of church life. It describes the church as "reformed and always reforming." For too many, the church was reformed at some point in the past but ever since has simply preserved that order. Yet the Reformers envisioned a dynamic church—one always alert to new possibilities, one that humbly understands that no set of reforms can ever produce an eternally perfect church.

The typical evangelical model of R/R has been dynamic too, but in a catastrophic way. Only modest changes are undertaken in an otherwise static condition until finally a decisively new movement tears open a new way forward. If the Reformers hoped their churches would be ever reforming, evangelicals later seem to have taken on a wrenching model of ever *converting*.

Many would argue that the church today, or some part of it at least, needs revolutionary change, and that may be so. But when that change comes, or in cases in which such drastic change is unnecessary, the Reformers' advice to seek *continually* ways to improve the church deserves to be heard. No important Christian leader, that is, has ever taught the "entire sanctification" of *the church* in this life, and Christians should not act as if their churches and traditions are already perfect and therefore not in need of important reformation.

Revival and Renewal: Who Wants It?

Christians have long debated whether revival and renewal can be expected from God if we do our part, or whether it is always a surprise of grace. But all have agreed that we are obliged to position ourselves so as to receive what grace God would bestow. Experts on the history and character of R/R such as Richard Lovelace and Howard Snyder offer valuable advice to the church in this respect. Several common elements emerge in their writings that point the way forward.

First, *prayer* is necessary, both individual and corporate. Lovelace, in his handbook *Renewal as a Way of Life,* puts the challenge bluntly: "If we are to be delivered from attempting only what is predictably achievable, we must return to a proper regard for prayer." Otherwise, he notes, "many worship services are monuments to the spiritual self-centeredness of local churches. It is a wonder that many pastoral prayers ever rise higher than the ceiling, when they so rarely embrace anything beyond the walls." J. Edwin Orr, a student of revival of a previous generation, believed that God will give us exactly what we request. And the apostle James provides the corollary: "You do not have, because you do not ask" (4:2).

Second, *community* must be built and sometimes rebuilt along new, healthier lines. In particular, notes Howard Snyder in *Signs of the Spirit,* small groups have been and continue to be vital in renewal movements. His historical study of Pietism, Moravianism, and Methodism demonstrates powerfully how small, dedicated groups of Christians attract and disciple new converts while they encourage spiritual keenness among more mature believers. Snyder concludes: "Every Christian should be part of a small committed cell group. . . . The small group is a basic structure which is universally, crossculturally relevant and necessary."

Third, *theology* clarifies and directs everything else that is done. R/R movements typically rediscover and freshly articulate classic doctrines of God, humanity, sin, salvation, sanctification, and hope. More than this doctrinal core, however, Christians need instruction in the dynamics of vital Christian life with God and each other in order to pursue together a clear and coherent vision of discipleship. The mission of the church is badly compromised by the blithe ignorance and culpable stupidity of Christians. Lovelace declares, "Warm hearts alone will not conquer a culture unless we wield the instruments that govern the central mindset of society: *ideas*."

Fourth, *mission* provides the crucial outlet for the energies that build up and are released in R/R. Indeed, committed engagement in mission often helps to foster and even spark R/R in the first place and then continually along the way. Lovelace again helps us with a striking metaphor. Churches are not to be "therapy centers" supporting Christians in their *careers;* they are to be "mission stations" supporting Christians in their *callings.*

Faithfulness must characterize the Christian church, however, whether or not God sends R/R its way. Of course, the church must discern whether a lack of spiritual potency is its own fault. It also must guard against defining spiritual health only in terms of visible, palpable results such as increased statistics, larger buildings, and proliferating institutions. These may not be present in a faithful Christian group, and they may well be present in an unfaithful one.

At last, and at first, however, is the most basic consideration of all. Revival, renewal, awakening, and even reforming all demand effort, time, humility, love, hope, faith, patience, and more. They are costly, and especially so to those deeply invested in the current shape of the Christian church. The crucial question is, Do we really want to change much at all?

PART 7

DENOMINATIONS

31

What's in a Name?

There are hundreds of denominations of Christianity in North America today and many thousands more around the world. Where do they all come from?

The proliferation of denominations has traced a sort of exponential upward curve during the history of the church. At first, there was just one church. By the year 500, several smaller groups had splintered off. By the year 1000 or so, there were two main Christian groups, Orthodox and Roman Catholic, with distinct varieties within each. By the next five-hundred-year increment, the 1500s, there were Orthodox, Roman Catholic, Protestant (mainly Reformed and Lutheran), Anglican, and Radical Reform movements (notably the Mennonite and the Hutterite). By the year 2000, there were thirty-four thousand types!

The First Millennium

The Christian church began in unity under the leadership of the Holy Spirit in Jerusalem. But the threats, advantages, and just plain realities of differentiation, if not division, appeared early on. In one of his earliest extant letters, the apostle Paul chastised a church for splitting into factions centered on particular leaders: "One of you says, 'I follow Paul'; another, 'I follow Apollos'; another, 'I follow Cephas'; still another, 'I follow Christ'" (1 Cor. 1:12 NIV). But as Paul's own missionary career shows, the ethnic distinction between Jews and Gentiles made for real differences in the first-century church (so Acts 15), even as they were bound together in mutual respect and concern (so the offering for the relief of the Jerusalem church [2 Corinthians 8]).

By the year 500, however, the church had experienced several important divisions. Some had occurred over certain doctrines such as the nature of the incarnation: The Nestorians and Copts, still important groups in the eastern Mediterranean, were expelled. Some groups left on their own to preserve, as they saw it, the moral purity of the church, with the Donatists of North Africa the most prominent of these. Some small groups, such as the Montanists, also questioned the emerging leadership structures of the church, preferring a more charismatic style of authority.

By the year 1000 or so, there were two major groups of Christians, divided along the same lines as the Roman Empire, which had earlier split into East and West. The Eastern church took the name Orthodox, which means both "correct doctrine" and "correct worship." It was actually a fraternity of regional and ethnic churches that each centered on a particular major city in the eastern Mediterranean area (such as Alexandria, Antioch, and Constantinople) and northeastern Europe (such as Kiev and, later, Moscow). The leaders of these major churches were called "patriarchs," and together they governed the church in accord with the statements of the first seven ecumenical or "whole church" councils. (These councils included those that issued the famous Nicene Creed regarding the Trinity in 381 and the Chalcedonian Definition of the nature of the incarnation in 451.)

The other major division of the church took the name Roman Catholic, emphasizing the unique leadership of the bishop of Rome and that denomination's claim to be the one universal (or "catholic") church—the former emphasis setting it apart from all other churches to this day. Since that time, Roman Catholicism has become the largest Christian variety in the world and has the same status in both Canada and the United States. The main outlines of its doctrine and church order were set out clearly for the first time at the Council of Trent in the sixteenth century as the church responded to the challenges of the Protestant Reformation. Since then it has refined but never changed its fundamental convictions. Especially since the "opening up" of this church in the Second Vatican Council (1962–65), however, increasing numbers of theologians, clergy, and others within its fold have been calling for change in its views on a wide range of issues, from the prohibition of artificial birth control to the requirement of male and unmarried priests to the uniqueness of papal authority itself.

The Reformation

By the year 1500, the Eastern Orthodox churches had suffered a great deal as a result of the militant spread of Islam. Constantinople itself had fallen fifty years before, and the center of Orthodoxy had long since moved to the "third Rome," Moscow. The Roman Catholic Church had suffered in a different way, becoming largely corrupt during the Renaissance and in dire need of reform. It had already incorporated a number of vital reform movements, however, from various monastic orders (such as the Benedictines and Cistercians) to the friars (the Franciscans and Dominicans). More recent and more radical challengers, however, had been expelled, such as the English Lollards under John Wycliffe, the southern European Waldensians, and the Bohemian followers of Jan Hus in the later Middle Ages.

The sixteenth century saw the Western church split into major traditions that mark it to this day. Almost simultaneously, the two main divisions of mainstream Protestantism formed under Martin Luther in Germany (hence Lutheranism) and Ulrich Zwingli in Switzerland (later called Reformed). At first, these two streams were as one, united in their commitment to the unique authority of the Bible (versus pope, councils, creeds, and traditions); salvation by grace alone through faith alone (versus faith plus works); and the freedom and responsibility of each Christian to act as priest to another (versus the mediation of the clergy). Indeed, the better-known leader in Reformed circles, the Frenchman John Calvin, always saw himself only as a disciple of Luther. (It is Calvin's prominence that leads many to refer to this type as Calvinism.)

Yet the two groups did split, largely over differing views of the nature of the Lord's Supper. To be sure, this was not sheer pedantry, for the Reformed position as articulated by Zwingli (namely, that the Lord's Supper is *only* a memorial using mere symbols of bread and wine) was so different from the Roman Catholic view of the sacraments (that they actually provide grace in the heart of the believer) that Luther and his friends feared they would never heal the breach with Rome if they allied themselves with the Reformed. The Lutherans held on to this hope of reconciliation for some time.

Even the moderating views of Calvin and others on the question of the sacraments and on other controversial matters failed to restore full relations, and these two versions of the Reformation went their own ways, working out similar but different views concerning a wide range of issues. In each case, the Lutherans were more conservative; that is, they made the least change from the Roman Catholic position. For instance, regarding church polity, the Lutherans retained the traditional structure of leadership by bishops, known as *episcopalianism*, while the Reformed preferred leadership by groups of elders both at the congregational and regional level, hence *presbyterianism*. The Scottish Reformed under John Knox took up this term as their badge, calling themselves Presbyterians.

The Reformed tradition thus was rooted in French- and German-speaking Switzerland and in Scotland. In the seventeenth-century struggle for Dutch independence, the Reformed faith became emblematic of resistance to Catholic Spain and became the established tradition in the Netherlands. Pockets of Reformed belief waxed and waned in France among the people called Huguenots. Emigration to America helped the Reformed faith expand to its modern dimensions.

For its part, Lutheranism dominated northern Germany and then became important in the struggles between kings, nobles, and merchant classes in Scandinavia, ultimately triumphing with the monarchical cause in all of those countries. Through emigration, Lutheranism came to North America. The vast majority of Lutherans now belong to either a more inclusive or a more conservative denomination. In the United States, the Lutheran Church in America is the mainstream variety, with the Evangelical Lutheran Church in Canada its northern counterpart. The largest group of more separatist Lutherans in the

United States is the Lutheran Church–Missouri Synod, known in Canada as the Lutheran Church–Canada.

The English church in the sixteenth century took its own distinctive course, also under the promotion of monarchs. King Henry VIII famously established a national church under his own leadership so that he could marry as he wished to promote his dynastic concerns. Henry had no love of Protestantism, but his move was one of the great ironies of church history because it opened the door wide to reform. Henry's children, Edward VI, Mary, and Elizabeth I, in turn switched the church back and forth between Protestantism and Catholicism, but finally Elizabeth's powerful and pragmatic hand established the shape of Anglicanism to this day. It was an inclusive church that embraced as many as possible. Its doctrine, articulated in its Thirty-Nine Articles, was a blend of Reformed and Lutheran emphases. Its polity was traditional episcopalianism. But the key to its common life was its worship, as set out in the Book of Common Prayer. Ever after, one was an Anglican if one confessed the Articles, respected the bishops, and used the prayer book.

These various forms of officially sponsored Protestantism, however, did not include all critics of the Roman Catholic alternative. A number of tiny groups emerged that sought to cut back to the root (Latin *radix*) of the church to reform it. Thus, scholars call them collectively the Radical Reformation. Many of these groups did not live out the century, but some did and established patterns that would have influence well beyond their own communities. Followers of the Dutchman Menno Simons (hence Mennonites) and Moravian Jacob Hutter (hence Hutterites) understood the church to be made up of believers only, that is, those who were capable of and had made a deliberate confession of faith and had undergone baptism as a mark of that confession. (Since almost everyone in sixteenth-century Europe had been baptized as infants, these Christians were pejoratively tagged Anabaptists, or "re-baptizers.") Their alienation from most of Europe—which, Catholic and Protestant alike, tended to persecute them as threats to social unity—encouraged them to turn inward and champion principles such as the separation of church and state and nonviolence in resolving disputes. They would traverse much of the world as they looked for places to settle in peace.

Mennonites and Hutterites today are divided into a variety of groups, mostly along ethnic lines and over the corollary issue of assim-

ilation that has affected most other groups—how much they have
adapted and conformed to more dominant forms of Christianity in
North America. Some, for instance, retain the communal ethic; others champion distinctive Anabaptist teachings without separate communities; still others have been so shaped particularly by evangelicalism as to have dropped the very term "Mennonite" from their
names.

Protestant Proliferation

Not everyone was content with the options opened up by the sixteenth century, however. Many in England, for instance, believed the
Reformation had not gone far enough and insisted that the church
be purified of any remaining Catholic features. These Puritans
annoyed Elizabeth and her successors because of their strident
demands, and they finally did away with their monarchical opposition in the English Civil War of the seventeenth century. Puritan religious beliefs regarding the importance of preaching, a genuine heartfelt conversion, and a disciplined moral life were embraced by many.
But the ironfisted policies of Oliver Cromwell soon alienated the populace, and the monarchy was restored. Yet Puritanism had already
begun to splinter as a religious movement. Once united in opposition to Anglicanism, they later found they disagreed with each other
over polity (English Presbyterians disagreed with those who saw the
individual congregation as democratically in charge of its own affairs
and came to be called Congregationalists), the nature of the church,
its sacraments, its relationship to the state (so the Presbyterians and
the Congregationalists were agreed on Reformed principles versus
the believers' churches of the Baptists)—and even mystical challenges
to the traditional importance of sacraments, preaching, and the
authority of the Bible itself (as in the case of the radical Society of
Friends, or Quakers).

As the seventeenth century gave way to the eighteenth, the
Lutheran church in Germany experienced renewal through a movement known as Pietism. Under the leadership of scholars and preachers such as P. J. Spener and A. H. Francke, Pietism championed a
warmhearted relationship with God that was nourished by Bible study
and small-group fellowship and that flowed out in service through

evangelism and a wide range of social ministries, from education to medicine. Some of these influences came to Canada through Lutheran groups and through the small Moravian church that embodied the Pietist impulse. But Pietism would be adopted by an Englishman with great effect for his own country and for North America.

John Wesley, an Anglican clergyman, encountered Pietist faith in a way that challenged his own and was powerfully transformed at one of their Bible studies in London. Wesley blended what he learned from them with the discipline he had developed in a small Christian student group at Oxford. In company with his brother Charles and another Oxford friend, George Whitefield, Wesley set out to bring the gospel especially to the poor and to revive the Church of England.

The way of the Wesleys and Whitefield had already been too rigorous for many Anglicans in their student days, and their "Holy Club" had been derided as "Bible moths" and, portentously, Methodists. But the message of the new birth, of conversion and assurance right on the spot through the grace of God as one put one's faith in Jesus, swept through England like wildfire. Wesley, following the theological tradition of seventeenth-century Dutch theologian Jacob Arminius (hence Arminianism), emphasized the importance of individual choice in salvation and straightforwardly called his listeners to exercise their wills and decide for God. His own theology made clear that no one could make such a decision without God having graciously brought their corrupt wills into a restored freedom. But at that point, individuals were indeed responsible, and Wesley preached to that responsibility.

Methodist chapels sprang up, and by the end of Wesley's long life, it was clear that the Anglican fireplace would not contain Methodism. Against Wesley's own original intentions, a new denomination formed, and it expanded dramatically into North America, becoming one of the largest denominations in both the United States and Canada by the middle of the nineteenth century.

Like most large movements, however, some of its original fire cooled, and the nineteenth century saw a number of groups emerge to champion the doctrine of Holiness, the idea that, once converted, the believer could come to know such perfect love (Wesley's term) for God that one would never deliberately sin again. Believers, therefore, should quest after this state, usually understood as granted all at once in a "second blessing."

The Church of the Nazarene, the Free Methodists, and other groups stood squarely in this tradition, and it influenced others as well. The Christian and Missionary Alliance, established by Canadian Presbyterian A. B. Simpson originally as a transdenominational mission in 1887, at first taught Holiness doctrines—more than it does now. The Salvation Army, another mission-turned-denomination, also got much of its early fire from the Holiness movement, which influenced its English founder, William Booth.

The nineteenth century gave birth to a radical impulse known technically as primitivism or restorationism. This kind of church sought to turn back the clock to the first century and live out a simple church life as the apostles were supposed to have done. Simultaneously and independently, in the British Isles the Christian or Plymouth Brethren were marking out lines remarkably similar to those emerging in the United States among what would become the Christian Churches and Disciples of Christ. The latter churches grew rapidly, especially in the United States. The Brethren, for their part, remained a small denomination on both sides of the ocean, but their influence has been disproportionately large in the evangelical community through support of transdenominational institutions such as Regent College and Inter-Varsity Christian Fellowship and through an extraordinary number of "alumni" leaders now serving in other denominations. The theology known as "dispensationalism," which has affected many denominations, first arose among the Brethren, particularly through one of its early leaders, J. N. Darby.

The Twentieth Century

The twentieth century saw two more major developments on the North American denominational scene. One began literally on New Year's Day of the new century in a Bible school in Kansas as a young student experienced the Holy Spirit so dramatically that she began to speak in another language. Pentecostalism was born, and it swept into Canada in its first decade. It carried on the Holiness emphasis on a second work of grace, terming it the "baptism of the Holy Spirit" (much to the discomfiture of other traditions!), and added its distinctive belief that this baptism was manifested invariably by speaking in tongues.

It was not so much this spectacular mark, however, but the undeniable spiritual energy of this movement that propelled it rapidly into the vanguard of missions and church renewal around the world. The largest single congregation in the world is Pentecostal, as David Yong-ghi Cho's church in Seoul, Korea, claims over one million members, and Pentecostalism continues to expand in Latin America, Asia, and Africa. Pentecostalism in Canada has remained remarkably united, with virtually all Canadian Pentecostals belonging to the Pentecostal Assemblies of Canada or the Pentecostal Assemblies of Newfoundland. In the United States, however, there are a welter of Pentecostal denominations, many of them also divided along ethnic lines: white, black, and Latino especially, but also Asian varieties including Korean and Chinese.

The Church of England, the Methodist church, and the Presbyterian church were the dominant denominations in English-speaking Canada by the turn of the twentieth century. In 1925, though, almost all of the Methodists and Congregationalists and two-thirds of the Presbyterians joined together to form the United Church of Canada. This was an unprecedented union of quite dissimilar traditions, paralleled later in India, Australia, and elsewhere. Its basis of union was largely Presbyterian orthodoxy, and its polity also retained the Presbyterian middle ground. It thus became Canada's largest Protestant denomination. On the American side, the United Church of Christ enfolded Anabaptist and Congregationalist traditions, while formerly divided Presbyterians and Methodists, previously riven by the Civil War as well as by strictly religious matters, joined to form major inclusive denominations.

The twentieth century saw a few splits in Canadian denominations. Perhaps most notable was the division within Ontarian and western Canadian Baptists that resulted in two major groups, the more conservative Fellowship of Evangelical Baptist Churches and the more inclusive Canadian Baptist Federation. The United States, marked much more by the fundamentalist-modernist controversy and by racial divides, saw many denominations splinter along those lines. But more commonly, division came as Canadian denominations separated from their American counterparts, whether small groups such as the Evangelical Free Church or quite large groups such as the Lutherans. Ethnic differences continue to mark Orthodox traditions and some groups such as the Dutch Christian Reformed, but most denominational differences along these lines are becoming fainter and may ultimately disappear (as among Mennonites and Baptists, for instance).

The enthusiasm for organic reunion of denominations seems slight these days, even in the face of tight budgets and declining numbers in many denominations and congregations. Recent arrivals on the scene, most notably charismatic groups such as Vineyard churches, remain quite small yet, but they diversify the array of denominations still further. North Americans may not make a proportionate contribution to the thirty-four thousand denominations worldwide, but we have not diminished this number much either.

32

Multi-denominationalism

American humorist Emo Phillips skewers Christian denominational chauvinism in a notoriously funny sketch.

A man is driving across a deserted bridge at midnight. Suddenly his headlights pick up the figure of another man, poised on the side of the bridge, ready to jump.

The driver immediately stops, gets out of his car, and begs the poor fellow to climb down.

"I'm a Christian," the driver implores. "Don't you believe God loves you?"

"Yes, I do. I'm a Christian too."

"Really? What kind?"

"Protestant."

"Really? Me too. Baptist?"

"Yep."

"Really? Me too. Northern or Southern?"

"Northern."

"Really? Me too. General Northern Baptist or Particular Northern Baptist?"

"General."

"Really? Me too. General Northern Baptist Hard Shell or General Northern Baptist Open?"

"Open."

"Really? Me too. General Northern Baptist Open Conference of 1847 or General Northern Baptist Open Conference of 1886?"

"1847."

"*1847?!*" With that, the driver gives the man a shove. "Die, heretic!"

I would like to celebrate again an idea whose time has come. It is an idea whose time has never left, and it is an idea rooted in the Bible itself. But it is an idea to which I would like to give a distinctly modern name: multi-denominationalism.

The more familiar North American term *multiculturalism* means different things to different people. I understand it to mean the ideal of people from a wide range of cultures bringing the best of those cultures to the common project of building a single but variegated society.

Native Canadians and Americans bring what they have. Quebecois and Cajuns bring what they have. Jews bring what they have, Scots bring what they have, Pakistanis and Chinese and Ukrainians and Trinidadians and Sikhs and Newfoundlanders all bring what they have to the common table of our national life in one country or another. We all share with one another and we all enrich one another out of our differences, in the mutual enterprise of a unified but not uniform nation.

Fuller Seminary president Richard Mouw reminds us that this ideal is a secular version of great prophecies of the Bible. In his unjustly neglected little book, *When the Kings Come Marching In: Isaiah and the New Jerusalem,* Mouw exposits the vision of Isaiah 60. The prophet sees "the wealth of the nations" flowing into Jerusalem, the glories of each land presented to God by the grateful rulers of every people on earth.

These different peoples do not cease to be different in God's city. They do not somehow transform at the gates into "generic humanity," into something other than brown or black or white, into someone other than African or Arab or European or Asian. They are different, and splendidly so. Yet they also are united in their desire to worship the one true God and to enjoy their common citizenship in the New Jerusalem.

This pattern strikes me as instructive for the differences within the Christian "nation." Differences among churches in a religion that has spread around the globe should be expected and affirmed as each new people receives and expresses the gospel in their own language and cultural forms. Differences even within ethnic groups can be expected as various personalities prefer different styles of music, preaching, and service to others. Denominations simply institutionalize these differences.

Some denominational divisions have been sinful, yes. But most reflect authentic, interesting, and important differences among God's people. What is scandalous is the attitude that says, "Our way is the only way and the complete way." The thoughtful Christian might wonder, in fact, if God has not deliberately withheld some goods from each church and tradition and given them to others in order to humble all Christians and remind us that only all together do we represent the body of Christ, the continuing manifestation of Jesus in the world.

The scandal, therefore, is not that there are Anglicans and Catholics and Mennonites and Presbyterians. The scandal is not that some churches like organs and others prefer keyboards and guitars. The scandal is not that some churches speak English and others speak French or Korean or Swahili. Each of these can be a colorful tile in the mosaic of the worldwide church.

Too often our attempts at ecumenism have been limited to projects in which we leave our denominational differences at the door. Parachurch organizations and other special purpose groups understandably encourage us to do so in order to cooperate in this or that important ministry to students, children, or the poor. But where is the opportunity to enrich each other with our differences? Where is the place in which we can ask the Mennonites to tell us about their distinctive witness to peace and community? Where is the occasion in which we can ask the Orthodox to tell us why they revere icons? Where is the opportunity to explore the Anglican Book of Common Prayer as a worship resource for other Christians as well? And where can we meet for the Salvation Army to teach us about care for the poor, for the charismatics to show us how to revel in the Holy Spirit, and for the Presbyterians to instruct us in thoughtful deliberation?

Sociologists of North American religion tell us that we are moving into an era of "post-denominationalism." If that's true, then I think that's too bad, for we will lose a lot of the color and vividness and spice and power of our denominational differences in favor of a few bland blends. What we need to leave behind is not denominations but denominational*ism:* the complacent conceit that keeps us from learning from one another, from giving to one another what we can.

So let's resist both denominationalism and post-denominationalism. And let's foster multi-denominationalism instead. It will bring blessing to the church and will model a new form of cooperation for our neighbors in our fractious countries.

PART 8

33

Some Sacred
Bottom-Line Thinking

North American evangelicalism faces twin crises in this first decade of a new millennium. The first is a leadership crisis, and the second is a funding crisis. A record number of Christian organizations seem to be seeking middle- and senior-level administrators these days, and a disturbing number are suffering financial trouble.

Leading publications in both Canada and the United States are struggling financially, with a wary eye on how the Internet is affecting them for better and for worse. And they keep looking for capable editors and publishers to help guide them through these parlous times.

New Bible schools, colleges, and seminaries continue to pop up, but a number of long-serving schools have closed or merged with others. Many of them face the daunting challenge of replacing senior officers—do you know any excellent deans or presidents you can recommend? A large part of the burden of those officers is steward-ing finances that seem perpetually to fall short of what is needed to fulfill the school's mandate. Moreover, no one should underestimate the strain of living on—and trying to hire and retain good workers on—what are generally meager salaries.

A number of leading Christian television broadcasters have been in deep financial trouble for several years now on both sides of the bor-der, and as the founders of some of these ministries age and retire, the question of succession looms large.

The word *crisis* comes from the Greek word for "decision," a fork in the road. As many shrewd leaders will admit, times of financial con-straint can be good for an organization: Troublesome or unproduc-tive personnel can be dismissed, misbegotten programs can be cut, extravagant expenditures can be reined in, and new priorities can be set with fresh self-understanding.

All of us who support such organizations with our money, time, and prayers are players in this serious game, and what we must do is both simple and drastic. We must prayerfully and informedly decide which organizations will live and which will die. It is our duty, in rev-erence before God and with determination to glorify him above all, to communicate to such organizations what their future will be.

We must recognize, in fact, that whether we do it prayerfully and informedly or not, we *are* deciding by giving—and *not* giving; by vol-unteering time—and *not* volunteering it; by praying—and *not* pray-ing. We are deciding which ministries will thrive, which will barely survive, and which will disappear. We are also deciding which new ministries will begin and grow.

So we must not be moved by advertising pitches aimed at induc-ing guilt rather than prompting respect and enthusiasm. We must not contribute merely because we have a friend or relative in such-and-such an organization. We must not support something just because it is local, spectacular, or denominational. Let's say out loud what we all know to be true: Some organizations are led by crummy boards that have hired inferior executives who preside over ineffective staff, and to give them one dollar more is just sending good money after bad. We each stand or fall before our own Master. We must decide with the counsel of the Holy Spirit how best to devote the money, time, and prayer we have at our disposal.

Do we need all the Christian schools we have in North America? Do we need all the Christian publications? Do we need so many

Christian student ministries? Do we have too few good leaders spread among too many organizations? Do we need *more* or *better* in any of these cases, and thus ought we to provide more support for such persons and their ministries?

Some Christian organizations that exist today will not live to see January 2010. In at least some cases, that's entirely a good thing, and perhaps more should be on the chopping block. But let us act on our responsibility before God to make sure that the *right* ones continue, and continue in robust health, with only the unproductive being pruned away.

34

By Their Honoraria
Ye Shall Know Them

When it comes to how we pay our spiritual workers, I am embarrassed to be a Christian. And you probably should be too.

A friend of mine is a gifted staff worker with a well-known Christian organization on a university campus. He is married with three young children and works hard and long at his job. Frequently, he is asked to speak at churches' youth retreats or special events sponsored by other groups. Rarely is he paid well for what is in fact overtime work.

One weekend he left his family to speak at a retreat for more than one hundred young people, each of whom paid to go away to a well-furnished camp for three days. My friend gave four talks and participated in a question-and-answer session—a typical and demanding schedule. But his work didn't end there, of course. Retreat speakers are "on call" all weekend: for impromptu counseling, offering advice over mealtimes, and modeling what they preach on the volleyball court or around the campfire. There is very little time for relaxation in that role, however restful the retreat might be for everyone else.

So at the end of this tiring weekend, at the close of the Sunday luncheon, the leader of the group thanked him profusely at the front of the dining hall (he had gone over very well). Then he tossed the speaker a T-shirt emblazoned with the group's logo while everyone clapped. It took my friend several minutes to realize that this shirt was his total payment for the weekend's work. He got in his car, without even a check for gasoline, and headed back to his waiting family.

An isolated and extreme example? Not at all. Every professional Christian speaker has stories like this one.

A widely respected author was asked to headline a fund-raising banquet for a women's organization. She prepared a talk on the subject requested, left her husband and children at home, drove herself in the family car across the city to the site of the meal, chatted with her tablemates, and then delivered her speech. Again, it was apparent from the applause and the warm remarks that greeted her when she took her seat that she had done her job well.

The evening ended, and the speaker was saying her good-byes. The convenor then appeared in a gush of appreciation. "Your talk was just excellent," she said. "Exactly what we wanted. Thank you so much for coming!" Then, by way of payment, she grandly swept her arm over the room and said, "Just help yourself to one of the table centerpieces."

We Christians have two problems in this regard. One might be remedied by an essay such as this one. The other can be fixed only by the Holy Spirit.

The first problem is that most people who invite speakers are not themselves professional speakers and so honestly don't know how much is involved in doing this work well. So let's price it out straightforwardly and consider whether we pay people properly in the light of this analysis.

A speaker first has to receive the invitation, work with the inviter to clarify and agree on terms (usually this requires correspondence back and forth), and confirm the date. Then the speaker has to prepare the talk. Sometimes a speaker can pull a prepared text out of a file, but usually at least some fresh preparation is necessary to fit the talk to a particular group and its context. (Let's remember that the speaker at some time did indeed have to prepare this talk from scratch, so the inviting group does have a share in the responsibility for that preparation since it will benefit from it.) The speaker concludes her preparation by printing out her notes and perhaps also preparing a photocopied outline, overhead slides, or PowerPoint presentation for the benefit of the group.

Next, the speaker must make travel arrangements and then actually travel. Most of this time is unproductive: Airports and airplanes are not designed to aid serious work (unless the inviting group springs for first-class seats and airport lounges—an uncommon practice), and driving one's car is almost entirely wasted time.

The speaker arrives and then has to wait for her particular slot. This time might be spent more or less pleasantly, depending on the situation, but it's hardly what the speaker would be doing if she had her first choice of options at home.

She finally gives her presentation, waits for everything to conclude, and returns home. If she is out of town, normally she will have to spend at least one night in a hotel room, probably sleeping badly in a strange bed and, again, spending time to-ing and fro-ing that is almost always unproductive.

Count up all those hours. Not just the forty minutes she actually spoke at the banquet or the four hours she was actually in front of the microphone during a weekend conference but the many, many hours spent in the service of the inviting group from start to finish. Divide those hours into the honorarium, assuming her costs are covered (!), and you have the true wage the group paid her.

One speaker I know was asked to speak at a weekend conference requiring of her three plenary talks plus a couple of panel sessions. She would have to travel by plane for several hours and leave her family behind. The honorarium she was offered? Expenses plus $300. Her husband heard of it and replied with a rueful smile, "*I* will pay you three hundred bucks to stay home with *us.*"

Here's yet another way to look at it. A speaker was asked to give the four major speeches at the annual meeting of a national Christian organization. He was also asked to come two days before the staff meeting in order to address the national board twice. In return, he was offered travel expenses and accommodation for himself and his wife at the group's posh conference center—of which they were extremely proud. So the speaker asked for an honorarium of $2,000 for the five days he would be away plus all the time he would spend in preparation for this large responsibility. The group's president immediately withdrew the invitation, saying he was charging too much.

Now, let's think about this. To get to the remote facility, the speaker and his wife would have to drive their car part of the way, then take a ferry, and then perhaps a float plane. The group clearly had no trouble covering considerable traveling expenses. The group was covering similar expenses for two dozen board members and well over one hundred staff members. The conference center was advertised in its glossy brochures as deluxe, and it looked that way in the photos.

So what would be the total budget for a weekend like this? Figure on, conservatively, 150 people with traveling expenses averaging $600 each (allowing for airfare across the country for most) plus accommodation expenses of at least $200 each for the long weekend. This comes out to a total budget of at least $120,000. Let's assume that the group offered the speaker some sort of honorarium—surely at least $500. This means that with a total budget of $120,500, this group disinvited its speaker because of a difference of $1,500—slightly more than 1 percent of its conference budget. Is this good stewardship by a Christian nonprofit corporation? Or is it something else?

One wonders about the "something else" when one looks closer to home and examines the typical honoraria given to preachers who fill pulpits when pastors are on vacation. Most churches now pay at least $100, although I know of many, including both mainline and smaller evangelical congregations, that still pay less.

Let us ask ourselves, before God, how we can justify paying a guest preacher a mere hundred bucks. He has to accept the invitation and become acquainted with the various duties he will have to perform. He has to prepare a sermon—again, even if he is going to preach one he has preached before, he still has to decide on which one to preach and then prepare to preach it well on this occasion. He has to travel to the church and take his place with the other worship leaders. He has to preach the sermon and greet people afterward. Then he has to drive home.

It's likely that he has invested ten hours or more. We offer him one hundred dollars, and that works out to ten bucks an hour—a little more than minimum wage. He has to pay all of the taxes on that, so now he's taking home perhaps sixty or seventy dollars. Is that what we think our preachers are worth?

Let's look at it another way. The average congregation isn't large, so let's suppose that two hundred people are to hear the sermon. By offering the preacher even $150 (which is more than most churches pay), we're saying that his sermon is worth less than one dollar for each person who hears it.

It would be worthwhile for those who invite speakers to their events to do this simple bit of division: Take the proposed honorarium and divide it by the number of talks, then divide it again by the number of people in the audience. The result is the price per talk per person. Is the talk you want your speaker to give worth more than, say, a scoop of ice cream or a chocolate bar?

Let's look at it still another way. Many Christian speakers have expertise that is in demand from secular agencies as well. Invariably, those agencies pay better, sometimes a lot better. A Christian psychologist I know has told me that he is paid at least one thousand dollars per full day of consulting with government agencies. He counts himself blessed if he is offered even half that much by a Christian group. Flip it around, and we observe that even we cheap Christians routinely pay high wages to our physicians, lawyers, plumbers, airline pilots, and other skilled people whose work we want done for us in an excellent fashion. Why don't we pay Christian speakers accordingly?

Some of us even self-righteously think that we shouldn't pay such people at all because they're doing "Christian" work or "spiritual" work and therefore shouldn't charge for it. The notion, however, that spiritual, theological, or other "Christian" expertise should not be paid for is utterly foreign to the Bible. From the Old Testament requirements that generous provision be made for the priests to Paul's commands in the New Testament that pastoral workers are worthy of their wages and should be paid accordingly (1 Corinthians 9), the Bible reveals that people in such occupations are worthy of both esteem and financial support. Indeed, we show our esteem precisely in the financial support we give them. We think our physical health matters, so we pay good money for good physicians. How much does our spiritual health matter?

Thus, we encounter the second problem, the one only the Holy Spirit of God can address. It might be that we have been paying Christian speakers badly because we have been unaware of all that is involved in preparing and delivering an excellent speech. Now that we know better, we should pay better. But the second problem of simply undervaluing such Christian service is in our hearts, not our heads, and the Bible is plain: We undervalue our spiritual teachers at the peril of undervaluing the divine truth they bring us. God frowns on such parsimony.

Indeed, God has threatened one day to mete out to each of us our appropriate wages for such behavior. Those wages will make even a T-shirt or a table centerpiece look pretty good.

35

Seven Deadly Signs

istoric evangelicalism has unblinkingly taught robust doctrines of both sin and sanctification. It has pronounced each human being born since the fall of Adam and Eve to be corrupt at heart, bent away from God's will and toward foolish self-interest. Evangelical theology has maintained that, unless God's grace intervenes, each individual person and each group of human beings will subvert and pervert the good order of God's world. And evangelicalism has then gone on—in the face of this dark portrait of original sin—to rejoice that God *does* intervene. God forgives people's sins, regenerates their hearts, and remakes them. As they cooperate in this difficult work of sanctification, God progressively transforms each one into the image of Christ and joins each to the other in a community of holiness and love.

In the late 1990s, the Institute for the Study of American Evangelicals (ISAE) completed a major investigation of the history of American evangelical use and abuse of money. These studies—conducted by more than two dozen scholars in Canada and the United States ranging over more than two hundred years of church life—warn us that we are not taking sin seriously enough in these matters. Our personal and professional financial habits are, in a word, *liberal,* and in the most superficial sense of the word: We think we're basically okay, and our organizations are basically okay, and our work is basically okay, so we don't need to guard against evil in any important way.

Look at what happened with the New Era scandal. Few of the organizations involved in this fiasco exercised what lawyers and executives call "due diligence" in making sure that the scheme was legitimate. Fewer still took seriously the Bible's warning that "the heart of man is deceitful above all things and desperately wicked" and so probed even further than standard business practice requires to be certain that God's money was going to be used properly.

One of the most important dynamics in that mess, in fact, was the interlocking relationships of board members of various Christian and other philanthropic organizations. These relationships naturally fostered respect and trust. In this case, sadly, that trust was sorely misplaced. Yet if the Christians in these positions of influence had taken the Bible's teaching on sin seriously, they could not have objected if their fellow Christians had wanted to investigate deeply enough to make sure sin had not infected the New Era venture.

Motivational speakers on the business circuit exhort their audiences to "plan to succeed." Inasmuch as this advice helps us to prepare properly for positive outcomes of our efforts, Christians can agree with this advice. But in the light of the whole counsel of God, we should also *plan to fail.* We can faithfully hope for God's blessing in our ventures, but we should also prudently prepare for the eventual emergence of evil.

Let us hear the inspired words of the apostle John about both sin and sanctification and apply them particularly to our financial arrangements at home, at work, and in all other ministry:

This is the message we have heard from him and proclaim to you, that God is light and in him there is no darkness at all. If we say that we have fellowship with him while we are walking in darkness, we lie and do not do what is true; but if we walk in the light as he himself is in the light, we have fellowship with one another, and the blood of Jesus his Son cleanses us from all sin. If we say that we have no sin, we deceive ourselves, and the truth is not in us. If we confess our sins, he who is faithful and just will forgive us our sins and cleanse us from all unrighteousness. If we say that we have not sinned, we make him a liar, and his word is not in us.

1 John 1:5–10

Most of us are committed to honesty in the abstract. Of course we are! None of us plans to deceive and cheat and steal. We *intend* to do the right thing all the time. It's only when the truth becomes uncomfortable, inconvenient, or even dangerous that we are tempted to lie, manipulate, and cover up. Yet life frequently confronts us with just such times of trial, and "if we say we have no sin," John warns us, we delude ourselves. We are wrapping our sin in the disguise of darkness and pretending that our finances are in faultlessly good order.

The apostle's imagery of sin and sanctification prompts us to consider the twin virtues of *transparency* and *illumination*. We need both to avoid anything that blocks God's sanctifying light in our lives and to seek more of that pure light.

About a decade ago, however, the board of a major North American college and seminary chose to remain in the dark for years while its incompetent president struggled to keep the institution afloat through bad loans and bad management. Board meeting followed board meeting; report followed report; audit followed audit. And no one on the board shook himself awake and said, "What's really going on here?" The banks finally blew the whistle on the overextended school and refused to lend it any more money. Only painful disclosure, under a new president and board, could restore confidence in this long-admired organization.

Our capacity to mislead others is exceeded only by our capacity to deceive ourselves. Here, then, are some warning signs for us, in our ministries, businesses, professions, and families, that might indicate we are hiding something in our use of money and might alert us to something bad that needs to be brought into the light.

1. You don't want to talk about a financial matter with your spouse, your subordinate, your boss, your accountant, or a donor. You always have a good reason to hold back, of course. Often it's with the best interest of the other person in mind—or so you tell yourself. But Christians must always ask, "Why, really, are we keeping this thing a secret?"

When an organization's salary scales are kept out of sight, for example, it is easy for suspicion to breed questions and doubts. Many Christian colleges have paid extra to faculty members in "hard-to-hire" positions, such as those in business, psychology, and computer science. Other organizations pay top dollar for development officers who will raise the money that pays everyone else's salary. Such decisions might be entirely justifiable in terms of the institution's own values. But if the administration won't come clean (an interesting expression, isn't it?) on its practices and motives, it is easy for others to worry that the organization is sacrificing community spirit and egalitarianism for pragmatism and efficiency.

On the domestic front, there are sometimes sound reasons for husbands and wives to maintain separate credit card and checking accounts—each can develop a personal credit rating, for instance. But too much separation of finances keeps spouses from sharing together in perhaps the most contentious issue in a household: money. The same holds true for children who have too much financial independence: It's a short step from privacy to secrecy, and secrecy shuts out the light of another's loving counsel.

2. It's been a while since someone in your organization or family has said no to you or told you that your suggestion is a bad idea. Now, unless you are always, *always* right, or unless your associates are too obtuse to recognize your shortcomings, you have established a dark environment in which no illumination can reach you from those who are closest to you. That means you can manipulate money without anyone else sounding an alarm until it's too late.

Over and over again, the ISAE research reveals evangelical churches and other ministries dominated by a charismatic leader whose unquestionable authority closes off the possibility of checks and balances on his use and abuse of finances. To prevent such a leader from stocking leadership positions with uncritical family members, the Evangelical Council on Financial Accountability (founded in 1979) has strict rules about nepotism. But in many Christian organizations, the dynamic is as obvious as it is unhealthy: We all need Mr. Big, for without him we have no ministry. So who wants to put her job on the line by questioning his judgment? Healthy organizations—from families to churches to corporations—must instead be structured in such a way that dissent can be heard without the dissenter risking disastrous reprisal from the thin-skinned.

3. You find yourself paying unhealthy attention to competition, whether other individuals, congregations, or organizations. You have to wrestle inwardly with envy of others' successes, and you are tempted to relish their setbacks. You tend toward "zero-sum" thinking regarding donations ("If it's going to them, it could have gone to us") and ministry opportunities ("If they get to do that instead of us, then our work is truncated"). If you pause to reflect, you can notice a pattern of criticism in your conversations about others, especially those in the same line of service as yours. The Bible calls such delicious chattering "gossip"—no matter how refined and pseudo-spiritual our phrasing of it may be.

Executives and pastors in particular are notoriously lonely people. Few of them—in our day or in the past—have sustained close friendships with those who could offer spiritual direction and comfort. Who counseled Jonathan Edwards? Who privately exhorted Charles Finney? Indeed, some biographers have suggested that Billy Graham has stayed on the straight and narrow so long and so well precisely because some of the good ol' boys from his youth, who remember when he was nobody special, have stayed his friends and confidants through the years. We all have needy egos, and we are prone to sin in order to satisfy the demands of those egos. We all need someone who will help us admit to the evil strategies we follow to advance our own interests at the expense of others. Or will we go it alone, making excuses to ourselves and others for our lack of accountability and assuring ourselves that no one else could really see things as clearly as we do?

4. No one on the leadership team of your church or organization is an authority on theology and ethics who can provide expert advice on thorny issues. The board instead is stocked with businesspeople and professionals who can contribute marketplace expertise, and wealthy friends of the ministry who can contribute, well, money. In many cases of ISAE research, leaders justified decisions with half-remembered snatches of Scripture ("The worker is worthy of his wages," or "Him who hon-

ors me I will honor") or, worse, with secular proverbs invoked as Proverbs ("Each generation should pay its own way"). No one is equipped to put questions into a broad and deep theological context that keeps various Scripture passages and Christian principles in proper balance. In such an environment, as historian David Paul Nord puts it, economic necessity too easily gets baptized as evangelical virtue.

5. Sitting alone at your desk or trying to fall asleep in your bed at night, you have a sour feeling in your heart, head, or stomach about your most recent purchase, or about your debt load, or perhaps about the fund-raising letter or annual report you have just sent out. You don't feel single-minded and pure but instead sense a nagging inner conflict that grabs at your insides and costs you sleep. Headaches, back pain, obesity, drowsiness, insomnia: Alarms are flashing! Psychologists call this phenomenon "somaticizing" (the Greek word for "body" is *soma*). We human beings are physical as well as spiritual, and we do well to pay attention to our bodies, which signal to us with physical distress that something is spiritually wrong.

Organizations and homes can "somaticize" too. Fraying carpets, dirty windows, broken window blinds, and poor lighting all point to a household or ministry under too much stress. At the same time, however, elegant furnishings, state-of-the-art equipment, and a high-end dress code can be the organizational equivalent of self-indulgent obesity rather than trim fitness.

6. As a supporter of or a participant in a church or other ministry, you recognize that your organization is under financial stress, and you are doing all you can—praying, fund-raising, cutting costs, increasing efficiency. Still, you are finding it difficult to pay the bills. Are you considering the prospect that institutions tend never to consider: that the time of useful service is over and the organization should disband?

Financial struggles are often tests of faith and shapers of character. As Dwight Moody once testified, "God has always given me money when I needed it. But often I have asked Him when I thought I needed it, and He has said: 'No, Moody, you just shin along the best way you can. It'll do you good to be hard up awhile.'" But unless we believe our organizations should go on forever, there must come a terminus sooner or later. The decline of financial support may be one way in which the body of Christ is communicating God's will for your ministry: scale down or even stop work. Are you transparent to this possibility and seeking more light on the matter?

7. You have apprehensions about a financial decision your superiors, church leaders, or fellow board members are making—and yet you cannot obtain enough hard, reliable information to evaluate this decision. Sometimes, of course, it isn't one's responsibility to know such things. But when people on legitimate levels of decision making are kept uninformed, or underinformed, something evil may be lurking nearby. Many institutions studied by the ISAE project were officially governed by people—trustees, presidents, elders—who were kept in the dark by defensive and sometimes even deliberately deceptive executives or pastors. So, too, have donors—who also have a trust from the Lord to steward their donations wisely—been misled.

We must beware the tactic of appeals to "trust," as in "Don't you trust me?" The biblical principles of transparency and illumination ought to inspire leaders to a sincere willingness to cooperate in any genuine investigation, a humble openness to correction from another, and a fervent desire above all to avoid sin and pursue holiness.

To enable this essential give-and-take to happen, there must be more than one channel of reliable information up and down the line. Yet most organizations, including evangelical ones, follow the typical organizational pattern of a single flow of information that passes through a crucial gateway managed by a single individual—whether the senior pastor of the church, the head of the department, or the CEO of the organization. Again, ISAE research shows that many boards have no more information to help them decide on the health of the organizations under their care than what a president or pastor decides to offer them. Donors, too, are presented with either glossy brochures or photocopied newsletters from an organization's public relations office, neither of which present adequately accurate and extensive information.

In short, some evangelical homes are run as if Mom and Dad are never wrong and can never be challenged properly by the children.

Even worse, some are run as if only one parent is infallible and cannot be corrected even by his or her spouse. Some churches are run as if the senior pastor or board chair alone should have all the facts and therefore make all the final decisions. Some Christian businesses and nonprofit ministries are run as if the leaders are not only omnicompetent, and thus could never make an innocent mistake, but also entirely sanctified, and thus would never sin against anyone. Structurally, therefore, there is little accountability for those leaders, even less protection of subordinates, and no real openness to dissent.

Commendably, some organizations have responded to this challenge. One seminary recently appointed an ombudsperson to a full-time position to take up the cause of any concerned employee. Many evangelical organizations make sure that employees are represented at the highest levels of decision making. In each case, these ministries are attempting to live and work in God's light.

Whom are we kidding about money in our lives and work? The apostle John reminds us that many of us are deceiving ourselves, as well as others. We are stumbling in darkness, and we need to repent right now. All of us need to take sin as seriously as the Bible does in every area of life, including our finances.

Especially our finances.

PART 9

36

One Does Not Equal Infinity, but One Is Infinitely More than Zero

G et a cause."

Some smart aleck had scrawled this graffito on an announcement posted on the bulletin board of a seminary I visited recently. The announcement described a meeting for women who were concerned about gender issues in the seminary and in the church community at large. The graffitist apparently was annoyed—and probably threatened—by the group and had tried to put it down.

But what a curious bit of sarcasm. At a seminary, of all places, aren't students supposed to learn what it means to be devoted to something beyond themselves? Aren't they supposed to learn about commitment to others, perseverance in truth, and how to press on toward justice and goodness in the face of indifference, resistance, and hostility? So why should it be uncool to "have a cause"?

We must allow that the history of the church is full of people who got hold of a single good idea and then championed it as the one, true, and worthy cause for everyone else to join. We are right to beware when someone says, "The most important problem facing the church today is . . . ," or "The one thing we all need to do is . . . ," or (my personal favorite) "The crying need of our times is . . ."

God's work is greater than any one cause. Or to put it better, God's one cause is the extension of his influence, his kingdom, into and over all the world, every corner of it. God's view is total, his resources infinite, and his ambition literally universal.

Our views and resources, however, are quite limited, and our ambitions must therefore be limited too. But because we cannot do everything doesn't mean we shouldn't do *something* and do it well. The New Testament repeatedly teaches and demonstrates that the church is made up of various people pursuing various callings under the single calling of God to glorify him in all things.

It is in this sanctified, mutually complementary sense alone that we can redeem the terribly individualistic phrase from the 1960s, "Do your own thing." My thing may not be your thing, but if I am obedient to God, I will pursue my calling with vigor and persistence while honoring your dedication to the task God has given you.

Let us listen carefully, then, to what God may have for us to undertake. It might not be central to the work of our family, friends, or fellow church members, but it might be God's will for us. And even a small amount of time and money invested in a girls' club, a scout troop, a food pantry, a Sunday school class, a pro-life chapter, a choir, a political party, a book group, or whatever it might be will enrich our lives and the lives of others much more than if we don't invest them there at all.

A little elementary mathematics appears as the title of this chapter: A single thing is not everything, but one is much greater than zero. One commitment faithfully and joyfully taken on for the glory of God—that's what each of us can undertake. In fact, as you'll recall from math class, one is *infinitely* more than zero.

So what?

So get a cause.

37

No More Mr./Ms. Nice Guy

I was once at Speaker's Corner in Hyde Park, England, where anyone who cares to do so can mount a platform and regale the passersby. One slight, bearded man was attempting to preach the gospel but was doing so in such a diffident and stuttery way that (I must confess) I quickly moved on to sample more impressive rhetorical offerings. Ten minutes later, as I returned, I saw that a small group of fifteen or so had now surrounded the little man on his milk crate.

Directly below him, speaking furiously into his face, was a younger man with a red flag pin on his lapel. As I came within earshot, I heard Marxist terms and slogans. The fellow was tall, good-looking, and obviously used to getting the best of any argument. The man on the milk crate looked down forlornly at this whirlwind at his feet, abashed by this vociferous adversary.

I listened to the Marxist's charges for about five or ten minutes. And then (and this will come as a tremendous shock to my acquaintances), I overcame my natural shyness and spoke up. I was prompted to do so by the most extraordinary charge I had ever heard against Jesus Christ.

The Marxist pounded a little New Testament he held in his hand and loudly proclaimed, "Jesus Christ was *not* a nice person! He called other people foul names and caused all sorts of trouble!" This insight had apparently stupefied the meek man on the milk crate and all those around.

So I suggested, in my mild way, "Well, *of course* Jesus was not a nice person!" The young Marxist whirled in my direction, clearly surprised.

I continued, "He called the religious leaders of his day the most terrible names possible in their vocabulary: 'sons of Satan.' He denounced the nation of Israel as deaf and blind to the revelation of their own God. And he promised hell to all those who didn't believe in him."

I finished: "*Of course* Jesus Christ was not a nice person. You don't crucify nice guys!"

Well, we set to it for the next fifteen minutes on Marxism versus Christianity. I'm glad to report that we parted respectfully when I had to move on and rejoin my patient wife and parents who stood quietly off to one side while I argued.

His initial gambit, however, has stayed with me ever since. Why did he think it such a telling blow against the Christian faith to expose Jesus as something other than a "nice" person? Why did no one else show up the silliness in this remark before I did?

I'm afraid it's because too many of us Christians want our acquaintances, above all, to see us as nice guys, and therefore we want our religion and even our Lord to be seen that way. I'm afraid it's because too many of us Christians are so worried about looking like those angry fundamentalists, those nasty TV preachers, those lunatic religious bigots that we have run too far in the other direction.

English writer Harry Blamires has suggested that the reason why most people in our culture don't care much about Christianity—as manifestly they don't—is that we never provoke them to consider it. There's nothing about us that confronts them with an alternative vision, another set of values, a different orientation.

So should we go out of our way to arouse resentment in some misguided zeal for martyrdom? Of course not. But our commitment to Christ and his kingdom ought to be such that those around us cannot help but see—in the day-to-day, decision-by-decision way we live and talk—that we're heading one way and they might be headed another.

What then do we make of Jesus' warning, "Because you do not belong to the world, but I have chosen you out of the world—therefore the world hates you" (John 15:19)? If the world does *not* hate us—does not resist us or despise us or fear us or mock us or challenge us—perhaps it is because it recognizes in us nothing very different from itself.

Jesus, however, provoked decision. Jesus was a razor slicing slowly through Israel, forcing people to one side or the other. Few who met him could remain blithely indifferent and undecided.

Jesus came to bring the bread and wine of communion, yes. Jesus came to bring the towel and basin of mutual service, yes. Jesus came to bring the new covenant in his own blood, yes and amen.

But Jesus also came to bring a sword (Matt. 10:34)—a double-edged sword that cuts between members of the same family, a sword that sets former allies against each other, a sword that cuts to the very heart of individuals and societies and makes them choose.

No, Jesus was not a nice guy. Jesus brought a sword.

Have we lost our edge?

38

"WWJD?" Is the Wrong Question

Many evangelical Christians in the United States and Canada are still enjoying the fad of wearing bracelets, T-shirts, and other gear emblazoned with the enigmatic symbol "WWJD?" "What Would Jesus Do?" is the translation, and thousands of people have found that this slogan helps them to focus on their commitment to Christ and to consider God's will more frequently as they negotiate life's decisions.

The "WWJD?" campaign, however, makes the same theological and ethical mistake made a century ago in Charles Sheldon's best-selling novel *In His Steps,* right down to the same phrase. And it's a mistake that makes this whole approach much less useful than it appears to be.

The ethical tradition of the "imitation of Christ" (as in Thomas à Kempis's classic devotional book) has a venerable heritage in Christian faith, and there is, of course, biblical support for it in several respects. The apostle Paul instructed his churches to "imitate me as I

174

imitate Christ." The Epistle to the Hebrews points to Jesus as our example of perseverance in trial. Christ himself in the Gospels bids his disciples to "follow me." And the classic text in this regard comes from 1 Peter: "For to this you have been called, because Christ also suffered for you, leaving you an example, so that you should follow in his steps" (2:21).

Still, let's consider a few things Christians affirm about Jesus that bear on whether he can serve, in every instance, as our example for behavior.

1. Jesus was, and is, divine as well as human.
2. Jesus was called to be the Messiah, a unique office in God's plan of salvation.
3. Jesus was Jewish, male, single, poor, and a full-time preacher who lived with a group of disciples and was on the road most of the time.

So we should refine our use of the example of Christ. Inasmuch as he models generic humanity in the service of God, he is our model: praying and worshiping regularly, loving God and his neighbor, seeking first the kingdom of God.

Inasmuch as he models God in the service of humanity, sometimes he serves as our example: washing each other's feet (John 13), putting others' interests ahead of his own (Philippians 2). And sometimes he doesn't: forgiving sins and issuing new revelation.

Furthermore, inasmuch as Christ models his own unique vocation, he provides us with an example only as we derive our calling from his: He inaugurated the kingdom of God, while we continue to extend it; he suffered for the sins of the world, while we also suffer, as his body, on the world's behalf.

The New Testament shows that Jesus' most intimate acquaintances—his mother, his brothers, his disciples—frequently failed to guess correctly "what would Jesus do" and even got in his way as a result. Jesus was full of surprises that look wise and even obvious in retrospect but were unexpected and even shocking at the time to those around him. We must be cautious, therefore, about claiming to know what Jesus would do in a given circumstance.

Instead, we need to take seriously Jesus' practice and teaching but also consider the time and place in which we each live and our particular callings both as members of the church and as individuals.

Jesus himself, when faced with deep questions regarding the will of God, didn't simply ask himself, "What would the Messiah do?" He carefully reviewed the Scriptures—knowing them so well that he could recite them. He consulted God the Father in prayer—sometimes spending whole nights in order to find clarity and conviction. He relied on the Holy Spirit to guide him from one thing to the next, however unexpected that would be. (We also enjoy the resource of consulting the wisdom the Spirit has articulated through his church throughout the centuries and continues to articulate in Christians today—if only we will make the effort.)

That's what Jesus did to decide what to do. And that's what we should do too.

39

Spending Too Much
on Those with Too Much?

I like Willow Creek Community Church. I've visited there several times, and I like much of what they do. I especially like their band: I still remember the unusually tasty arrangement they played of "Great Is the Lord" as an oscillation between jazz waltz and rumba. (Kids, don't try this at home.)

I like the churches I have visited in both Canada and the United States that have similar standards and objectives. They present high-tech, high-polish, and high-comfort sights, sounds, and spaces to those who are used to such things. Such churches pay attention to every detail, and everyone works hard to serve visitors in Christ's name.

Other innovators are spending lots of money, time, and talent on new ways of communicating the gospel to our distracted Palm Pilot/Nintendo/4WD contemporaries. Snappy billboards catch the attention of drivers and transit riders. Glossy leaflets, newspaper advertisements, and Bibles with trendy covers all manifest a commendable Christian concern to be heard through the clamor of popular culture.

But something nags at me a bit about all of this effort. When I look at Jesus' evangelistic career (I've been reading the Gospel of Matthew of late), I see that he doesn't seem to go out of his way to approach people who are preoccupied by "the cares of this world."

Yes, Jesus calls to rich Zacchaeus, but Zacchaeus is already looking for him. Yes, he engages the woman at the well, but she is hardly an upscale socialite planning her next soirée. Yes, he dines with Simon the Leper, but during the meal Jesus reserves his blessing for the nameless woman whom everyone else condemns for her unseemly breach of etiquette.

I wonder: Are some of us spending a great deal of God's resources to try to attract the attention of those who are successful and contented by the world's terms, when Jesus himself came not to the "healthy" but to the sick?

Sometimes I'm reminded of students in our high school Christian fellowship who connived desperately to get the student council president or football team captain to attend our meetings. That would give us status—as it brought glory to God, of course. These same people ignored and even slighted the less popular students—let's face it, the "losers"—who were grateful to belong to any club that would have them.

To be honest, I myself would rather hobnob with—I'm sorry! I meant "witness to"—confident, witty sophisticates. But I see few of them in Jesus' company in the Gospels.

I recognize that some worthy evangelistic theories advocate targeting leaders—whether Campus Crusade's strategy to win the big men and women on campus, or the time-honored missionary goal of converting the tribal chieftain—in the hopes that the rest of the group will follow. Still, I wonder.

Does God want us to devote so much of our creativity and effort to attract the attention and the fair-weather esteem of the dazzled, preoccupied, and complacent? Or should we concentrate on welcoming those who know that they are needy, those who would come in if they knew we wanted them, those who would likely receive gladly any grace we would give them in the Lord's name? How many of our God-given pearls are we presenting, with all the cleverness and charm we can muster, to ungrateful and uncomprehending worldlings who despise the gospel riches we offer and prefer instead the sensual plea-sures of the trough?

Yes, God loves the wealthy. (Since I myself count, in global terms, as one of those, I'm very glad he does.) Yes, God loves yuppies. Yes, God loves even those who think they have no need of him. And Chris-tians who are their neighbors must love them in God's name.

All I'm asking is whether we North American Christians are mak-ing the most of the opportunities we have. It's one thing to chase hero-ically after the errant sheep that are not yet in the fold. To mix both metaphors and parables, it's quite another thing to work so hard to entice indifferent swine while neglecting those who would joyfully accept what we offer—if only we would look their way.

40

Feminism Fatigue

Aren't you getting tired of feminism?

I remember when Anita Hill, of the infamous U.S. Senate hearings for Justice Clarence Thomas, was on our university campus a few years ago to raise our consciousnesses about sexual harassment. In a time of severe budget cuts, it was rumored that the Students' Union paid her $17,000 for her single speech.

At about that time, the same public university's central administration granted all female professors an across-the-board increase in base salary, while the faculty in general had to threaten to strike just to fend off an across-the-board *cut*. The "equity" committee was challenged: Did they really think that every female professor had been paid less than she should have been? Could they possibly prove such a thing? The committee's statistics themselves also turned out to be wrong. Yet the increase was not canceled: It was just scaled back.

A major newspaper ran a front-page story recently about a male civil servant who was thrown out of a government-sponsored session on sexual harassment. It was not because he had uttered a sexist remark, much less engaged in harassment. It was because he questioned the *premise* of the presenters that men everywhere are prone to violence.

Not long ago an acquaintance of mine told me that she had decided to withdraw from the second half of a university course in women's studies. She was fed up because the female professor, in the student's words, concentrated far too much on bashing men and not enough (ironically) on studying women.

Watch TV. Read the press. Aren't you tired of the special privileges given to women on the sole basis of their sex? Aren't you tired of the portrayal of all men as incipient rapists and of all women as long-suffering saints? Aren't you tired of—to put it bluntly—all the whining?

For the record, I'm a feminist. But I'm an old-fashioned feminist. I just want women to be treated fairly at home and in society at large. I just want men to have no special privileges on the basis of sex. I just want the discrimination to stop and for us to get on with a productive and happy coexistence. I don't have a bra to burn, I don't hate men, I'm not a lesbian: I'm a feminist.

My wife is a feminist too. But it's strange how she never gets tired of the subject of feminism and sexism, while I sometimes do. Sometimes, frankly, I think she goes on too long about it. She seems to be overly sensitive about things and makes too big a deal about stuff that, hey, just happens.

- Such as the board meeting of a Christian organization at which some of the men (including me, I confess) dominated and several times interrupted or ignored our softer-spoken female colleagues.

- Such as the protest of a gifted Christian pastor I know who, twenty years ago, complained that even then he was "tired of the 'women's issue'" and who still refuses to use inclusive language in his sermons: For him, "humanity" is still "man," and every generic personal pronoun is "he."

- Such as the frustration of a student who confided to me on the city bus that her Indian parents were furious with her because she was not already married and a housewife at age twenty-one and that her boyfriend's parents had forbidden him to see her because she wasn't the correct sort of Muslim. Both sets of parents want an arranged marriage and certainly not a marriage of these two young lovers.

- Such as the experience of the university sexual harassment officer who told me that there are professors (both male and female) who are still abusing their students with unwanted suggestive language, requests for dates, and even fondling during lab work. Another official told me that a senior professor had threatened to withdraw a foreign student's research grant if the student did not coerce his wife into a sexual liaison with the professor—and the student acquiesced.

My wife doesn't get tired of feminism. Now that I think about it, North Americans whose skin isn't white don't get "tired" of racism either. They get nauseated by it. They get exhausted by it. They get infuriated by it. But they don't suffer the mild annoyance, the "compassion fatigue," the wishing-it-would-all-go-away-and-leave-me-alone feeling that comes to people like me, privileged white males who don't know and can never know what it's like to have to deal with sexism or racism over and over again.

Does this mean that we should rally around every cause, every initiative, and every policy that claims the banner of justice? Certainly not: There are many agendas, some of them evil, that are promoted under this flag. But real injustice persists, the struggle is not over, and human beings who are loved by God are suffering each day because of prejudice and pride.

When it comes to justice, the Word of God is clear: "Let us love, not in word or speech, but in truth and action" (1 John 3:18). "If a brother or sister is naked and lacks daily food, and one of you says to them, 'Go in peace; keep warm and eat your fill,' and yet you do not supply their bodily needs, what is the good of that?" (James 2:15–16).

Only some of us will be called to a primary vocation of combating sexism. But each of us is called to do what he or she can, in his or her particular areas of influence, to promote justice and peace in this respect, as in every other respect.

If you're too tired to act as a feminist, I'm afraid you're just a comfortable sexist.

41

Summertime Stupidity

As readers of this volume have doubtless concluded, I am normally mild, reserved—even diffident.

But for this topic I have to make an exception, because we simply have to consider a truly amazing coincidence that will lead us to a dramatic principle of church non-growth!

What are the three months of the year in which North American churches typically are at a low ebb? You know, no Sunday school classes, no clubs, no choir; guest preachers most Sundays; everyone taking turns going on vacation? Yep, that's right: mid-June to mid-September.

Now consider this fascinating question: What are the three months of the year in which most people move to a new place? Ask any moving company: It's (hold your breath) *mid-June to mid-September!* (Cue trumpet fanfare over rolling tympani and crashing cymbals.)

So if we want to keep people from joining our cozy little church fellowship and thereby wrecking the nice thing we've got going here, one of the best things we can do is (and here is the dramatic principle of church non-growth I promised you) to make sure summer church is as dull, awkward, and repellent as possible.

My wife and I have changed cities five times, so we have a good deal of experience in checking out new churches in the summer. Out of this rich data base we have scientifically formulated some surefire tips for alienating summer visitors, which we offer here for free to those of you who don't want visitors ever to come back:

1. Change the time of the worship service, but don't change the time announced on the church sign, bulletin, telephone answering machine, or newspaper advertisement. That way newcomers will show up way too early or way too late, embarrassed and inconvenienced. They won't make that mistake again!

2. Have inadequate child care and preferably none at all. Cram sixteen kids from seven grade levels into one large room with one or two well-meaning but overwhelmed adults or—even better—thirteen-year-old girls who have yet to complete a baby-sitting course. Then watch the eyes of newcomers bug out as they arrive at the door and behold this chaos. Another good idea is to make sure that no one staffs the nursery so that tired parents of infants who have struggled to get to a new church on time (see tip 1) get to spend the entire service tending their children in a strange place. It's best, of course, simply to offer no child care at all so that parents can try desperately to look after their children in the pew or out in the narthex for the entire meeting.

3. Make sure that all printed materials are outdated, referring to last year's schedule of activities with no indication of what's to come in September. It's better, of course, to have no printed materials at all so that newcomers have no clue as to the life of this congregation beyond the immediate service. But if you're going to have them, then use last year's stuff throughout the summer. After all, there will be new material in September, when the members need it. Who cares about autumn in the middle of July? Those who need to know will eventually find out, right?

4. Maintain a casual, folksy, intimate—even sloppy—attitude all summer. Make sure the accompanists are new to your church and unfamiliar with your services, thus playing when they're

not supposed to, or at the wrong tempos, or in some other distracting way. It's best, of course, to make sure they're simply not very good, making mistakes while they play, especially during preludes and postludes.

5. Those presiding at the services should be equally inept, with poor speaking voices and obvious confusion as to the order of service. Have them grin when things go wrong as if it's just one more cute little thing we all enjoy.

6. Children should be encouraged to run amuck (see tip 2), with parents shrugging and smiling as they pull little Susie off the piano bench during a hymn or as they finally retrieve little Jason from his third lap around the sanctuary.

7. Ushers should run out of bulletins early and sit down as soon as the service starts so that latecomers will be utterly at a loss when they reach the sanctuary door.

This insouciance will help you feel fine about the strikingly poor quality of every aspect of the service and will encourage newcomers to form the important conclusions that (1) it's like this all the time, and (2) we prefer it this way! Whatever happens, don't apologize for any screwup and suggest that things are better in September. Those pesky visitors just might return!

As the poll data and denominational membership reports all suggest, our congregations are simply overrun with visitors clamoring to be admitted to our churches. So we have got to build barriers every way we can. Summertime stupidity—that is, having the worst possible church services during the peak relocation period—is a really good start! *Get planning now!*

42

The Importance of the Local

After Jesus' ascension, the disciples must have looked like a sorry bunch as they made their way down the hillside of the Mount of Olives. To say that they were a small, defensive group utterly without influence would be almost to *understate* the case. What could be expected of such a little group?

Less than three hundred years later, however, the Roman emperor himself would adopt Christianity, and the entire Roman Empire would fall into line behind him. However much the joining of church and state together under Constantine and his successors was a mixed blessing for Christianity, there is no question that his support of the Christian religion marked considerable success in the spread of the gospel outward from that lonely Judean hill.

Over three centuries, the gospel spread both horizontally and vertically throughout the Roman Empire. By the end of the classical era, there were Christian churches in every major city and in every province, and there were Christians in every stratum of Roman society. Christianity may have begun among the relatively poor, powerless, and oppressed (although even in the Gospels it is clear that some persons of influence were converted as well), but over three hundred years it claimed adherents—even under the sporadic but intense persecutions of this era—from bottom to top.

The story culminates late in the third century and early in the fourth. We know that Constantine (d. 337) adopted Christianity after the famous Battle of the Milvian Bridge in 312 and made Christianity legal in 313 in his Edict of Milan. Immediately before his reign, however, the church underwent the most widespread oppression it had ever experienced: the program of scapegoating under Emperor Diocletian (245–313) that the Christians called the Great Persecution. In the light (or perhaps "shade") of this event, Constantine's victory and support of Christianity looks positively miraculous: from darkest night to brightest day.

For all the ferocity of Diocletian's decrees, however, the Christian church did not disappear. As historian W. H. C. Frend notes, "The Christians were too well organized, too widespread, and too numerous to be destroyed." Indeed, most ironic of all was the fact that Diocletian and his "deputy emperor" Galerius were themselves married to women suspected of Christian leanings. The faith had spread, in fact, to the imperial family itself. Rather than being a dramatic reversal, then, the conversion of Constantine can be seen as simply the next and last logical step in the utter permeation of the Roman world by Christianity.

How did this happen? How did the shaky faith of a little band of Jews become the dominant religion of the entire empire? We are inclined to look at the noble missionary heroes of the New Testament: Philip, Peter, John, Silas, Barnabas, and, above all, Paul. However grateful we ought to be for these men, though, we must be careful not to misrepresent them. This was small-time evangelism: no media campaigns, no tents or stadiums, no P.A. systems, no choirs, no celebrity guests. Instead, there was a lot of tramping about, in ones or twos or threes or fours, conversing and preaching in homes and synagogues and marketplaces—even prisons. The only "mass-evangelism campaign" we know about from Acts happened right away at Pentecost, and we hardly think that everything went downhill from there, do we?

Not at all. Scholars of the early church have concluded that the gospel spread so far and so fast because of local initiative. It spread because ordinary Christians lived out their faith and took it with them as they moved around the empire. We have stellar examples right in the New Testament in Priscilla and Aquila, who lived in Pontus (Asia Minor—Aquila's home), Corinth, Ephesus, and on two different occasions in Rome. Indeed, even enemies of Christianity such as Celsus (a pagan philosopher of the second century) praised the high morals of Christians.

To be sure, the church owes much to the itinerant preachers, the pioneer missionaries and church leaders who traveled all over the Mediterranean world: from Asia Minor to Spain, across the top of Africa, and from Arabia to the British Isles. (The Mar Thoma churches in India credit the apostle Thomas with their founding, and this tradition may have historical support.) Leadership matters a great deal, and without the guidance of apostles, prophets, pastors, and teachers, the early church would not have spread so far nor have overcome its many problems.

It remains true, however, that the spread and vitality of the church depended mostly on the faithful leadership of "small-time" itinerants and local, "ordinary" Christian witness. Similar stories fill volumes of church history. Whether the monastic reforms of Bernard of Clairvaux (1090–1153) and the similar work of Francis of Assisi (1181/2–1226), or the reforms of individual cities by the Protestant Reformers in the sixteenth century, almost every significant movement of renewal and expansion of the church began *locally* as gifted leaders and willing workers invested themselves in small but worthy projects.

Another angle brings another aspect into view. The Evangelical Awakening, which brought the gospel to so many in England during the eighteenth century, arose out of the faithful but ignominious preaching of George Whitefield and the Wesleys as they stood up to their ankles in the mud of fields and crossroads. Refused the privilege of pulpits, they preached where they could. Small-time indeed! Yet we now understand that the roots of this revival go back further, in one case to an unhappily married Christian woman who determined to succeed in one particular local project. "There are few [persons], if any," she once wrote, "that would entirely devote above twenty years of the prime of life in hopes to save the souls of their children, which they think may be saved without so much ado; for that was my principle intention, however unskillfully and unsuccessfully managed." How grateful so many of us are, though, that Susanna Wesley persevered in her calling as mother to that family and to John and Charles in particular. Her child-rearing was one "limited undertaking" that had unforeseen but immense consequences for millions.

Another turn brings another issue into focus. Mordecai Fowler Ham (1877–1961) was a fiery American evangelist in the stereotypical Southern mode. He preached against evolution, communism, and the "liquor interests" and prided himself on "skinning the local preachers" if they didn't support his causes with equal vigor. Ham claimed one million converts at the close of his career and was awarded a doctor of divinity degree by Bob Jones College, but few today would recognize his name. His work apparently could never be compared with the other notables mentioned so far. He scarcely seems to belong in the same company with Bernard, Francis, Luther, or the Wesleys. Yet of those many converts he claimed, Ham could be especially pleased with one, for this virtually unknown evangelist was the instrument by which one young Southern boy came to faith in Christ, William Franklin Graham, Jr.—known to the world as Billy Graham. If Mordecai Ham had been used by God to make only *one* convert, this would have been a pretty good one to make. This would have been another kind of very profitable "local ministry."

We modern Christians, especially evangelicals, however, like things big. Big events. Big projects. Big institutions. Big budgets. Big personalities. As much as we take pride in our particular localities, we parallel the general culture as we tend to admire those who have "made it" nationally or internationally. (Compare, indeed, the common phrases "local hero" and "the big time.") We must be aware that this attitude poses several dangers to us and to our work with Christ.

First, if we are preoccupied with the hugely impressive, we can wait around for someone, somewhere, to take some grand initiative to solve our problems and meet our challenges. Why don't our denominational leaders help us, for instance? Why don't they give us money, or at least tell us how to raise money, for a new church building? Why don't they provide better Sunday school materials? Why don't they show us effective programs of evangelism and social ministry? Why doesn't somebody "big" do something?

Well, one might ask in response just why *we* don't do something. Our problems and challenges generally are local, and *we* are local, so what are we going to do about them? We can read good books and attend valuable seminars offered by experts that will furnish us with tools. But ultimately it is *we* who must discern God's plans for our church; *we* must determine the goals and objectives; *we* must draw up the programs; *we* must pray and think and study and teach and grow; *we* must do what is to be done.

The second danger associated with our preoccupation with bigness is that we will fail to support, perhaps even to notice, the worthy work that is already being attempted around us locally. We may ignore and even despise fresh initiatives of worship, fellowship, or ministry in our own church or local community because they do not have affiliation with or the stamp of approval of a widely recognized figure or organization. Yet which eminent national organization sponsored John Wesley and George Whitefield? What imperial or papal approval could Martin Luther have produced to validate his work? What major foundation provided the start-up funds for the Franciscan order? What prominent mission board sent out the apostle Paul? Let us then look around us for those who right now need our local support.

The third danger is that we will look down on ourselves. We will think *less* highly of ourselves than we ought to think (cf. Rom. 12:3). In the view of our heavenly Master, all our work, every day, is pleasing to him as we offer it up as faithful service. We are part of his truly grand project, and he weaves the threads of all our lives into a work of art that has eternal significance and beauty.

This glorious vision of our work fitting into a great pattern, however, may not always help us get out of bed in the morning to go to work, much less get out of bed in the middle of the night to attend to a crying child. At times we can rejoice in God's great symphony, but often our own parts still seem pretty minor.

C. S. Lewis reminds us, however, that things are not always what they seem and that *people* especially are not always what they seem. "It is a serious thing to live in a society of possible gods and goddesses," he writes, "to remember that the dullest and most uninteresting person you talk to may one day be a creature which, if you saw it now, you would strongly be tempted to worship, or else a horror and a corruption such as you now meet, if at all, only in a nightmare." The sturdy Reformation doctrine of vocation teaches us that God values all our work as it is performed according to his calling. The famous preacher is no more to be praised than the faithful slave.

So far, so good, perhaps. But what Lewis tells us, in concert with the testimonies of Susanna Wesley, Mordecai Ham, and so many others, is that our apparently little service may in fact turn out to be of unimaginable importance after all—in this world, possibly, but certainly in the next. We must see, furthermore, that Susanna Wesley and Mordecai Ham properly tried to convert the Wesley family and the young Billy Graham—*whether or not* those converts would become influential—simply because they believed that each individual is terribly important.

We have at least a sense of that even now, from a highly personal point of view, as we look back on those who have given of themselves to us in the past. Parents, relatives, friends, teachers, coaches—however wide their influence, it carries on through the years, never lost, as it marks each of us forever. To you or to me, at least, those persons' local ministries cannot be denigrated or forgotten, for their influence continues within our very selves, and we are deeply grateful for them.

We must see that renewal movements wax and wane, denominations come and go, and institutions of all sorts will not outlast the earth itself—but *we will,* and so will all of those whom we influence every day, right around us. The importance of our daily faithfulness within our families, with our friends, and in our occupations cannot be measured by human reckoning. But one thing seems sure: It is not little.

Can we therefore take care of our part of God's vineyard and trust God to make of our efforts what he will? Let's have the courage and the wisdom to think small and local, for in doing so, we concentrate properly on the eternal.

John G. Stackhouse, Jr. is a graduate of Mount Carmel Bible School, Queen's University, Wheaton College Graduate School, and The University of Chicago. He currently serves as the Sangwoo Youtong Chee Professor of Theology and Culture at Regent College and as Adjunct Professor in the Department of Classical, Near Eastern, and Religious Studies at the University of British Columbia.

He is the editor of three books of theology for Baker Academic and the author of five, including *Canadian Evangelicalism in the Twentieth Century: An Introduction to Its Character* (University of Toronto Press); *Can God Be Trusted? Faith and the Challenge of Evil* (Oxford University Press); *Evangelical Landscapes: Facing Critical Issues of the Day* (Baker Academic); and *Humble Apologetics: Defending the Faith Today* (Oxford University Press). In addition, he has published more than four hundred articles, chapters, and reviews in both scholarly and popular journals and books.

His journalism has received five awards from the Canadian Church Press. He currently writes a column for *Faith Today* magazine and serves as Contributing Editor to *Christianity Today* and *Books & Culture* magazines.

John Stackhouse lives with his wife and three sons in Vancouver, Canada.